As Light Lingers

Basking in the Word of God

As Light Lingers

Basking in the Word of God

by Nina Atcheson

Safeliz

Book design by Felicity Thomson
Edited by Tim Lale

Library of Congress Cataloging-in-Publication Data

This book was produced in cooperation with the Ministerial Association of the General Conference of the Seventh-day Adventist Church.

Editorial Safeliz, S. L.
Pradillo, 6 · Pol. Ind. La Mina
E-28770 · Colmenar Viejo, Madrid, Spain
Tel.: [+34] 91 845 98 77 · Fax: [+34] 91 845 98 65
admin@safeliz.com · www.safeliz.com

Book website: www.aslightlingers.com

ISBN: 978-84-7208-669-2

March 2020: 2nd print of the 1st edition
Printed in Thailand (IMP01)

*"Then Jesus spoke to them again,
saying, 'I am the light of the world.
He who follows Me shall not walk in darkness,
but have the light of life.' "*—John 8:12

To bask: To lie or relax in a pleasant warmth or atmosphere.—*Merriam-Webster* dictionary

To linger: To stay in a place longer than necessary because of a reluctance to leave. To spend a long time over (something).—*Merriam-Webster* dictionary

Endorsements

I just finished reading the book *As Light Lingers* by Nina Atcheson, and I love this book so much. This book not only gave me tools to understand the Bible better but also inspired me to read it more. It is a powerful tool, and I highly recommend it to everyone. The book has been such a blessing to me that I am planning to use it in my classes on spiritual growth.

S. Joseph Kidder, *Professor of Christian Ministry and Biblical Spirituality, Andrews University*

A year ago I discovered something fresh and new from a book about how to be baptized daily by the Holy Spirit. That book changed my life and ministry. This new book by Nina Atcheson may do the same for you. How can you separate the daily baptism of the Spirit from a daily, fresh reading of the Bible? Nina's strategic plan may be new to you—but if you implement it, you'll never be the same again. That's the Author's promise.

Dwight K. Nelson, *Senior Pastor, Pioneer Memorial Church, Andrews University*

Our daily walk with the Lord is so vital—it is the essential element in life. Many times we fail to provide the needed connection with the Lord in a practical way. Nina Atcheson has developed a meaningful approach to allowing the Word of God to become real on a daily basis. The General Conference Ministerial Association is nurturing the reading of this important work. You will be benefited by this personal approach to obtaining God's blessing through the reading of His Word.

Ted N. C. Wilson, *President, General Conference of Seventh-day Adventists*

Nina's love for Scripture is contagious. As you read her words, you'll want to read His Word again. And if you're still learning how, Nina will gently take you by the hand and help you.

ANDY NASH, *Author, 'The Book of Matthew: Save Us Now, Son of David'*

As Light Lingers is deeply moving as well as practical and is sure to revive your Bible study time! Nina Atcheson has obviously been gifted by the Holy Spirit in her writing of this beautiful book. I used my highlighter often while reading and was convicted afresh of my own need for a much deeper experience in God's Word. I look forward to sharing this resource widely!

MELODY MASON, *best-selling author of 'Daring to Ask for More: Divine Keys to Answered Prayer'*

If you are thirsting for a vibrant, refreshing, and meaningful experience with the Word of God—the Bible—you will find wise and practical counsel in reading *As Light Lingers: Basking in the Word*. Nina Atcheson shares very convincingly about the power of God's Word, challenging the reader to confront the main distractors that tend to keep the Bible hidden away from our lives. She presents an approach to the Bible which, if followed, will make the study of the Scriptures a personal, desirable experience. Feeding on God's Word with the help of the Holy Spirit is enriching, positively impacting the reader for spiritual revival and reformation. I sincerely recommend this book to all who desire to have the Bible as a true lamp in the pathways of life. This is great reading for youths and adults, written in a language that is easy to understand. After reading this book, I have been inspired to reorganize my Bible study and start over again.

GEOFFREY MBWANA, *General Vice-President, General Conference of Seventh-day Adventists*

I love this book. It's easy to read and so relevant, not only to individuals of any age or stage in their faith journey but also for families so that kids can also learn how to meaningfully study the Bible.

TERRY JOHNSON, *President of Greater Sydney Conference, Australia*

Nina Atcheson's book reminds me again and again that the key to spiritual growth and power is in spending time with God in His Word. We know, "Eternal life is to know God," and that doesn't happen without quality time spent with Him. This book underlines the importance of studying the Word prayerfully, inviting and allowing the Spirit to change you and use you according to God's will. It is filled with many profound spiritual lessons and also practical, specific advice on how to study it and implement it. I believe all pastors, leaders, and lay members will be blessed by reading it.

PAVEL GOIA, *Editor, Ministry Magazine*

This is a splendid book filled with wise and thoughtful insights that will encourage you to make quality time with God's word a priority in your life and which provides many practical tips and examples regarding just how to do so.

JOHN PECKHAM, *Professor of Theology and Christian Philosophy, Andrews University*

This is a wonderful, down-to-earth book. I like it because it is practical and not just theoretical. I believe this is an excellent tool to use with children and teens when we can teach them to dig deep into God's Word. This book is definitely valuable for families and children's ministries leaders and teachers all around the world.

LINDA MEI LIN KOH, *Director of Children's Ministries, General Conference of Seventh-day Adventists*

Atcheson calls us to foster a personal relationship with her best friend, Jesus. Spending quality time in deep personal Bible study is an essential part of knowing Jesus. In our busy, tech-driven lives, she shows each of us how to move past a cursory relationship—just going through the motions—to a personal and loving commitment and communion with God. I highly recommend this book to everyone who longs for that type of relationship.

LARRY BLACKMER, *Vice-President, North American Division*

Reading the Bible and spending time with God is not just about reading a chapter of the Bible and saying a quick prayer and we are done. It is dwelling in His presence and letting God wrap us in His love as we listen to His voice: the Bible. Nina has done an exceptional job of teaching how to do this. Praise God for how He has led her! This is a book to read and reread. What is so exciting is that she shares how her children are doing it too! This book will be a classic to pass on to many others until Jesus comes.

JANET PAGE, *Associate Ministerial Secretary for Pastoral Families and Prayer Ministries, General Conference of Seventh-day Adventists*

Nina Atcheson urges us not to let devotional books rob us of the beauty of simply reading or listening to the Word of God. Whether you prefer written contemplation or oral reflection, we can all receive the blessing that comes from meditating on what the Spirit, through God's Word, is personally and practically saying to each of us in these last days. Atcheson is right – a consistent devotional life is non-negotiable – for an individual, a couple, and a family.

JEFFREY BROWN, *Associate Secretary, General Conference Ministerial Association.*

After reading this book, I wish I'd had access to information that this book shares when I was younger, when establishing my faith in God. It provides practical kingdom principles for the pursuit of a closer relationship with God. Reading this book has reinforced that I can have a relationship with God that is not based on rules, but getting to know God more through the Bible.

EDDIE WILLIAMS, *Australia's Strongest Man, 2018*

Nina Atcheson, a mother and educator, has written an inspiring book on studying the Bible. Those who may have neglected reading Scripture for various reasons will appreciate the practical suggestions for finding joy in the text, suggestions that Atcheson has personally and successfully tried. Her writing is accessible and full of warmth, making one want to pick up the holy pages once again and read! Parents raising children will be especially encouraged. This is a highly readable and meaningful book.

JO ANN DAVIDSON, *Professor of Systematic Theology, Andrews University*

Foreword

We have been told that our greatest need is a revival of true godliness among us. The message in this book is crucial for each of us to have such a revival.

My heart "burned within me" as I read and then read again the pages of this powerful book by Nina Atcheson. The Holy Spirit was impressing on me the ways He has led me into this same beautiful experience with the Lord through His Word but also that I need it so much more deeply and consistently in these coming last days! And Satan will do anything he can to keep us from the time and tools needed to do it.

The Bible, God's living Word, gives us conversion, wisdom, victory, Christ-likeness, revival, love relationships, comfort, instruction, guidance, and joy—for it is the true "bread" we need to live fulfilled lives every day. How I resonated with what Nina says about all the "good activities" (and some not so good) on which we spend our spare moments each day instead of fortifying our minds and characters for the last battles before us. This activity leaves little time to have a clear mind for God's words and our relationship with Him.

You will not only be challenged by the message in this book and inspired by Nina's testimonies but also walk away equipped with many practical methods and helps for your life.

I believe this book is a "must read" for every man, woman, young adult, and even every child who desires to know Jesus personally through improving their life-changing, living experience—by immersing themselves in God's Word. Whether you're not sure what you believe, whether you're a new Christian or a lifelong follower of Jesus Christ, you will benefit from reading and applying the principles in this book. Every pastor, elder, teacher, parent, and church leader especially needs this book to help in the discipleship of not only themselves but also their families, church members, and even the people they need to reach in their communities.

I also am convicted that this extremely practical book can help us nurture and retain new members as well as longtime members, which is one of our biggest needs in every culture around the world. Please read this book! You will be blessed!

JERRY PAGE, *Ministerial Secretary,*
General Conference of Seventh-day Adventists

Contents

Acknowledgments

Above all, I am thankful to God, who has given us His Word—to love on us, to guide our lives, and to bless our future. This Word is His message, and all glory is His!

I am also truly thankful to these people:

My precious children, Jacob, Tahlia, and Eli, who each show me what it means to have childlike faith and to study the Bible openly and searchingly. You bring joy into my life more than you can imagine. I love you *immensely*!

My best friend and husband, Matt, who has patiently encouraged me to write this message, amidst our full life. Serving God and nurturing our family alongside you is the greatest and most wonderful privilege.

My sweet mum, Nerida Koolik, whom I've seen read her Bible every morning since I was a little girl, and my wise dad, Peter Koolik, who shows me what a life of abiding looks like through his selfless work. You both continue to inspire me to think of others and live for Jesus.

My dear late grandfather, Pastor Henry Miller, who, when I peeked through his home-office door as a child, would be bent over his desk, studying his Bible.

My beloved sister, Tatiana Green, and Jo Ann Davidson, John Peckham, and Joseph Kidder, who each gave of their time to encourage me and give their feedback on the book manuscript.

Pastors Jerry and Janet Page, who have prayed for me, provided feedback on this book, and opened up opportunities to share this message. What a blessing you continue to be!

And my extended family and the many others who have challenged me over the years to seek the jewels in God's Word.

1

The Unwrapped Gift

I gave my five-year-old son a birthday gift, and his little hands grasped it with delight. He held it for a moment, and I could see that he was wondering what was beneath the beautiful wrapping. He paused and shook it, hoping to find an answer to this question.

When this action gave no indication as to the package contents, he could contain himself no longer. He tore the paper away, revealing a family board game that I was sure would bring many hours of bonding and enjoyment to our whole family. But his face dropped when he saw what was inside. It wasn't what he had expected or hoped for. I could tell that it didn't seem valuable to him. My heart felt a little sad when I realized it wasn't what he wanted.

Then he asked an unexpected question. "Mummy and Daddy, could you wrap it back up for me? I don't want it right now. Wrap it up and put it beside my bed for another time." He turned away, eager to see if there was another gift to open.

This experience struck something inside of me. Do we act the same way toward God when it comes to His gift, the Bible?

Do you have a copy but prefer to keep it wrapped up, somewhere within reach but unopened, because there are seemingly better things to open or "play with" in your time? If your answer is "Yes," then you are not alone. In recent years I have opened this precious gift, and I can't help sharing with you what I have discovered.

What Are You Reading?

A friend who knows how much I love to read asked me what book I'm reading at the moment. "The Bible," I replied.

She gave me a funny look and responded with silence.

As I thought about this short conversation, I wondered a few things. First, why did my response stop my friend in her tracks? Was this really such a strange answer? I read a lot, but at the moment I'm really, truly reading my Bible in a big way. Second, why would the Bible not be a book I would want to read? It's the most published book in the entire world in any language, and one of the oldest. People have copied it in secret, smuggled it, paid big money for their own personal copy. Many have even died for it. If, indeed, it has been so precious throughout earth's history, surely it would be no less precious to me today.

Then my sweet friend, after looking blankly at me for a moment, replied, "I think the Bible probably is a good book. I just never know where to start. I know God can communicate through the Bible, but it's never really happened to me."

Have you ever felt like this, that if only you knew where to turn in the Bible, maybe you would find strength and hope from the words in its pages? Maybe you'd like to read the Bible but don't know where to start. Or perhaps you think you *should* be reading it, so you commit to reading a chapter a day (perhaps hurriedly, before your day begins), but life gets busy, and you can't stick to doing it for more than a few days at a time. Although I grew up in a strong Christian home, this was my experience. I can relate to you if it's yours also.

One thing I know for sure: someone wants to keep us away from God's Word: the enemy of God. He knows that when we read the Bible, I mean *really* read it, it will change our lives—and even the lives of those close to us. The devil does all he can to keep us from opening the pages of God's inspired Word. Maybe you know some of his tactics. Do your thoughts resemble these?

- *I'm too busy right now. How can I possibly find time to read the Bible?*

- *Life is too full, and I'm always so tired. When I open my Bible, I just doze off.*

- *I can't help it—I get distracted and drift off. I think about other things whenever I try to read the Bible.*

- *The Bible is out of date and irrelevant. It doesn't have anything meaningful to say about what I'm going through right now.*

- *It feels like I've heard it all before—the same stories or passages; what more could I possibly learn?*

- *I'm just not a reader.*

- *Deep down, I feel a little inadequate reading the Bible. I have not lived the way God wants me to, so He can't speak to me through His Word.*

If you've had any of these thoughts, you're not alone! These are some of the lies the devil whispers to stop us from opening the pages of life-giving power that will change us forever. We all hear these lies from time to time.

But God is waiting, gently knocking at the door of our hearts (Revelation 3:20), longing to spend time with us if we will just give Him the chance. And when we drink from His fountain, we'll hunger and thirst for more of what He offers. He will fill us, and we will be blessed beyond measure (Matthew 5:6).

Perhaps you have a vibrant relationship with Jesus right now, and maybe you know what it's like to search for and claim the treasures in the Bible every day. If this describes you, I'm sure you've seen how the Bible can speak straight into your life to give you guidance and peace. No doubt you've held on to promises and seen God work around you and within you in incredible ways.

Or maybe you've never experienced this. Maybe you see the Bible as an outdated book that is more a symbol of religion than something that can speak into your life today. Maybe you've read it in the past (or even today), but it doesn't seem "alive" to you, and your relationship with God feels stagnant or even nonexistent at the moment.

The truth is, right now God's Word is living, waiting for you to open it to speak to your heart, to encourage you, to challenge you, and to give you guidance for your future. It's available to you right now.

You don't need to be a scholar to understand it. "As in earlier ages, the special truths for this time are found, not with the ecclesiastical authorities, but with men and women who are not too learned or too wise to believe the word of God." [1] The Bible is not just an academic book or a collection of fables but a beautiful, profound account of how the Creator God of the universe seeks to draw us close to Him. It's a book that is amazingly "living." You can read the same story or passage time and time again and still see new truths or different truths that speak directly to your life.

Basking in the Light

We live in a dark world right now, and the enemy wants to keep us in the dark, as far away from God as possible. If you get up in the night without turning on a light, you may stumble because you can't see clearly. You can't see who or what is around you. When it's dark, your other senses are heightened, and it's easy to instinctively feel nervous or afraid in the dark. Instead of being rational, you may focus on your fears and magnify the unreal and feel scared or cold or alone.

In contrast, when you stand in the morning light, when the sun warms your very soul, it's easier for you to feel relaxed and happy. You see everything around you clearly—both beauty and pain. You see others, and you see the road ahead.

Jesus tells us that He is the light of the world (John 8:12). He can shine into the dark crevices of our lives and our world to make things clear and to "warm" us up from being tepid or lukewarm (Revelation 3:16). The Bible says that God's face actually shines and that His face can shine on us (see Numbers 6:24–26; Matthew 17:2; 28:3; Psalm 80:3, 7). After Moses came down from speaking to God, his face shone for days afterward because of the time he had spent with Him (Exodus 34:29–35).

As I thought about my desire to revive my relationship with God, I realized that this simply could not happen unless I spend high quality time with Him. And so I keep asking myself two questions:

1. How can I bask in God's Word, relaxing in His warmth and enjoying time with Him?

---

1. Ellen G. White, *Christ's Object Lessons* (Battle Creek, MI: Review and Herald Publishing Association, 1900), 79.

2. Do I linger with God? Do I stay with Him longer than what seems necessary because of my reluctance to leave?

The more I started to think about these things, the more God has put them on my heart. I earnestly believe that many of us need to be challenged to spend more time with God in His Word (me as much as you!), whether you've grown up a Christian or not.

I started to think about some really practical, intentional ways that we can more deeply know the Giver of this book and why I believe so many of us leave this book unopened. As I started intently studying my Bible, things began to change in simple ways. As I started showing my children how to study their Bibles, our home changed. These are the things I want to share with you.

As I write, I am praying that the Holy Spirit will speak to you and that you will know of God's longing to sit down and talk with you through His Word, and the incredible way the Bible will change your life when you read it. I believe the Bible will answer every question, every challenge, every worry, and every joy that is on your heart right now. And I pray that ultimately, your relationship with God will deepen beyond what you ever thought possible.

Before we continue, I invite you to pause. Take a moment and pray a simple prayer. Ask the Holy Spirit to speak to you as you read this, to give you an open heart so that God can speak into your life. I'm praying for you now, in advance, as I write this.

2

Enemy Lines

Events of vital importance are taking place around us;
we are on Satan's enchanted ground. Sleep not, sentinels of God;
the foe is lurking near, ready at any moment, should you become lax
and drowsy, to spring upon you and make you his prey.
Ellen G. White, The Great Controversy

Kukla, our Burmese cat, was the most snuggly pet in the world. She was my writing companion. She sat on my lap, followed me to the kitchen when I needed a snack, and meowed at me when she was hungry. We kept her indoors for the first six months of her life because the Michigan winter was too cold for her to be outdoors. When spring came, she would see us go outside and watch us longingly through the window.

One day, we decided that it would be fun to take her outside with us. The kids thought about making a leash for her, but we dismissed that idea and just let her roam while we followed closely behind. She was enthralled with the outside world—the new feel of grass beneath her paws, the sounds of the birds overhead, the new experience of wind and bright sunshine on her fur.

After that first day, having experienced the world outside, she wanted to be out in every spare moment! And we obliged. We watched her enjoy her newfound freedom until one day she delivered a chipmunk at our back door. We were shocked and upset! The lifeless body lay on the grass, and then my sweet, heartbroken children went and buried the little body under a tree. This was only the first of Kukla's days as a hunter. Every morning she would give a guttural *"me-o-o-o-w-w-w-w"* until we let her outside. It seems ironic that our sweet kitten turned into an aggressive killer. It seemed almost unbelievable when we saw her curled up and purring by our fireplace in the evenings that she could seek to kill and destroy helpless animals in the daytime.

Although people often blame God for all the evil in this world, perhaps it's worth considering what the Bible tells us about Satan. It says that he became a fierce hunter as a result of his choices. It describes him as a cunning, patient lion who not only waits to pounce on us but seeks to devour us (1 Peter 5:8). He watches and waits until he knows our weakness, and then he makes plans to strike with the intent not just to harm but to destroy when the moment is right.

Satan's #1 Strategy

One of the most significant attacks Satan can make on you is to stop you from spending time with God in His Word. Keeping people away from the Bible, in whatever way possible—whether through apathy, busyness, tiredness, or doubt—is, I believe, his number-one strategy in the lives of Christians today.

We are told that "Satan employs every possible device to prevent [people] from obtaining a knowledge of the Bible; for its plain utterances reveal his deceptions."[1] This is why it seems so hard to bask in the Bible—to make time and commit to it! Satan uses *every possible device* to stop us from reading God's Word. He knows there is power in it that makes him powerless. He knows that prayer and the Bible are the most powerful weapons that humankind can use against him, and he does everything he can to stop you and me from reading it.

The devil knows that if he can keep us away from the Bible for prolonged periods of time, he has practically won the battle. Satan knows that God's words are powerful and that they not only spoke this world into existence (Psalm 33:6) but can raise the dead (John 11:41–44) and expel temptation (Matthew 4:1–11). By keeping God's people away from their Bibles, he affects not only our relationships with God but our other relationships as well. Our marriages become strained, we yell at our kids, and we don't have enough patience with our friends or coworkers.

---

1. Ellen G. White, *The Great Controversy* (Mountain View, CA: Pacific Press Publishing Association, 1911), 593.

Life seems too busy, and we feel stressed, with no outlet, and burdened, with no solution.

We don't often pause to think about this or even recognize it is happening. Maybe we even think we're close to God, while days can pass by, even weeks, without our opening God's Word, and we are spiritually weakened more each day. Perhaps we say a quick prayer here and there and go to church, but do we open our Bibles and make it a priority to read it? We have moments of feeling close to God, but they don't last. We try to be good, moral people based on society's standards, but an emptiness remains inside of us.

Being distracted and not spending significant, high quality time with God has been a challenge for me over the years. When my children were very young and I worked in the evenings, it seemed almost impossible to make time for God. I was run off my feet with the wonderful but tiring job of caring for my kids in the daytime, followed by evening work at home, and restless nights followed by waking up to the kids. At times it felt as though I was in a spin cycle of busyness that I couldn't step out of.

During this time I realized I needed God's help the most. I needed patience and love more than ever as I sought to raise my young children to know Him. I needed Him, and although I would often pray to Him while rushing around with the children, it seemed near impossible to spend any amount of decent quality time in His Word. I felt an emptiness in my soul, particularly because it seemed I hadn't listened to a sermon in church for years because of the need to care for and train young children.

I talked to my husband, Matt, about this challenge, and in desperation I begged God to show me how I could be with Him more.

Then one day He gave me an idea. I dragged myself out of bed to the waking sounds of the children, gave them breakfast and read them a story, gave them some books and toys, and then I took my Bible and a journal and sat in my antique red chair in the corner of the sitting room. I started to pray openly, asking God to show my children that I was spending time with Him and asking Him to bless any small portion of time I had with Him.

Then I started to read. It wasn't very peaceful because the kids were not far away, but it was time with God. For the first few mornings, when the kids interrupted me or wanted me, I told them I was spending time with Jesus and that they needed to let me have that time just with Him without interrupting me. In hindsight, I see that although my children were quite young (two to four years old), over time they came to understand that when I sat in that red chair with my Bible, I was spending time with my best friend, Jesus. Now that they're older, I believe that it was important for them to see me making time for Jesus and modeling this to them.

Do you have a "red chair" somewhere in your life that you could go to as a symbol of a time and place where you can meet with God in His Word? The challenge of time is something many of us face. If you are a mother with young children, I want to encourage you to go to God and ask Him to help you find a way to make time with Him a priority in your life. If you are a busy businessperson or a full-time student, I encourage you to go to God with your challenge of time. Time with Him fills our souls as nothing else can, and it changes how we parent or lead or follow too!

There are other very real distractions. For a time, I was distracted by online shopping. I would surf the internet for good deals, for pretty clothes, things I thought my children needed—anything, really. I was still fulfilling my role as a mother as I should, but I often felt a pull to see what was for sale online, what new things I could find—fashion, homewares, and of course, what people on social media said they were buying.

After a while, in the back of my mind I realized I wasn't reading my Bible or praying much at all. At first, I dismissed this thought, and then I justified it. But eventually, I acknowledged that shopping was becoming a bit of an addiction for me. I prayed about it and tried to surrender it to God. I didn't want it to consume me as much as it was. I felt a little out of control. I tried to surrender, but the next day I would find myself back where I was before—seeing advertisements pop up beside my emails and, without realizing it, surfing the internet, not necessarily buying anything but looking for things I would buy if I could. My time was eaten away.

I felt annoyed at myself. How could I allow this distraction to consume me this much? I thought I was surrendered to God, yet it seemed as though this was controlling me. It was keeping me out of my Bible and off my knees. I would surrender and ask God to help me, and then very soon I would be back to where I was just a few moments earlier. I couldn't understand myself. Why couldn't I be stronger? Why couldn't I just remain surrendered, especially when I wanted God to help me?

Then something became clear to me. I was relying on my strength instead of God's. I was focused on my actions, not God's. I could never do this in my own strength. My human effort was worthless in the process. I had a desire to overcome but couldn't follow through.

All I needed all along was Jesus—a really meaningful relationship with Him. I couldn't just make a good relationship with Him happen instantly; I needed to *choose* to spend time with Him. I needed to *choose* to be with Him. I needed to *bask in His words* for me and *respond* to Him. I needed to give Him *my time*. I needed Him more than I needed anything else.

I realized that God's Word itself would be my greatest help in overcoming my personal challenge. Every morning I started to claim, out loud, God's promises—His words to me, and my prayer response to Him. Incredible promises like this one came to mind:

> The steadfast love of the LORD never ceases;
> his mercies never come to an end;
>   they are new every morning;
> great is your faithfulness. (Lamentations 3:22, 23, ESV)

I started praying the Word of God and claiming the Word of God. Have you ever done this? It's powerful! As part of your prayer, you speak a Bible verse to God as your prayer to Him. You tell God what's on your mind and heart and come to Him in humility, saying, "You tell me here in Your Word that [whatever you found] . . . , and I claim this as my prayer! Please do this in my life!"

It's important to carefully consider the words you read in Scripture and not take them out of context to manipulate them for your desires. However, God promises that His words will not return to Him empty:

> So shall My word be that goes forth from My mouth;
> It shall not return to Me void,
> But it shall accomplish what I please,
> And it shall prosper in the thing for which I sent it.
> (Isaiah 55:11)

This verse is one of my favorite promises in the Bible. It tells me that God's word is so powerful that it will change situations and lives and will make people prosper. No wonder Satan wants to keep me away from it! Yes, the enemy is doing all he can to take us away from being in God's Word, because he knows how it will change us.

We know that online shopping is not bad in itself; it's one of the great conveniences of life. I shop online when I need something that I can't easily get at my local store. But I'm now conscious of not letting online shopping consume me for hours and hours. I'm conscious of not allowing it to take away time with my family because the amount of time it had been consuming and how it was affecting my thoughts became unhealthy. I wanted God to bless my time as a mother, wife, friend, and sister.

Like me, you may be distracted with something that isn't bad in itself, and it might be absorbing your thoughts and time so much that you feel distracted and inadequate to go to God or to open your Bible.

Maybe your every spare moment is consumed with social media. Maybe you can't resist that subconscious action to reach for your phone to check the latest updates, and it seems to dominate every spare minute you have.

Maybe it's watching movies or TV. You're in the habit of watching something every night, and it's all you can think about all day.

Maybe it's gaming. You might be part of a group that plays together, and you like having that social connection, but it's taking so much of your thoughts and time that there's barely anything left for God.

Maybe it's food. All you can think about is what you might have for your next snack, and your eating is getting out of control. You're stressed, and your natural response is to go to food.

Maybe it's sports. Your body is a machine, and you are driven to exercise for many hours each day to achieve the goals you've set for yourself.

Maybe you're consumed with watching sports to the point that your thoughts and plans revolve entirely around which game is coming up next.

Maybe study or work takes every spare moment, and it feels impossible to give God any of your time because you have so many pressures weighing on you.

While these things are not wrong (in fact, some of them are very good), what I'm talking about here is overconsumption and an imbalance, where there is little time for God or people. I think we all struggle with something, and this something can leave little room for Jesus, even though we're told that life will be so much easier when we seek Him first (Matthew 6:33).

Consider this: "Satan well knows that all whom he can lead to neglect prayer and searching of the Scriptures, will be overcome by his attacks. Therefore he invents every possible device to engross the mind."[2]

Satan knows he has to pull out everything he's got in the time we're living, right before Jesus returns. His goal is to keep us from praying and reading the Bible, and he does everything possible to consume our minds to keep us away from God. We might be committed Christians, yet if we're not abiding in God through His Word and through prayer, we gradually wither inside. I know what this feels like, and you may, too. Distraction is Satan's best tool to keep God's people apathetic and powerless.

Jesus understands our apathetic condition even though He rebukes it (Revelation 3:14–22). Although He is God, He was also a human being who felt tired (John 4:6). He felt the pressures of life and escaped them by going away alone to pray to His Father (Luke 5:16; 6:12; Mark 1:35; Matthew 14:23). Jesus knew that time with His Father was the best thing He could do to regain strength.

I've spoken to children who love Jesus with all their hearts, but no one has ever shown them how to study their Bibles. It seems obvious to them that they'd start in Genesis and read from cover to cover, but it's easy to read for the sake of reading and then get disillusioned when you reach Leviticus. When you were a child, did anyone show you how to study your Bible and how to take something away from your reading that builds not just *what* you know but *Who* you know?

I've spoken to teenagers who are busy with school, who are grappling with their place in this world, who are searching for meaningful relationships. God isn't high on their agenda, and even if He is, how does one hang out with Him, anyway?

I've spoken to single professionals who are very successful in their areas of work, but their work swallows them up, and it seems there's no time to be with God daily.

I've spoken to busy moms and dads who are so exhausted from parenting that, for them, Bible study is the last thing on their minds. It's hard enough getting five hours of sleep a night, plus keeping up with housework, work, and the significant relationships in their lives, so it seems impossible to find an extra portion of time to give to God each day.

2. White, *The Great Controversy*, 519.

I've even spoken to some leaders who keep plugging on and yet are depleted more and more as time passes by because they don't have time to be in God's Word.

I've felt it myself in my busy-but-good life, doing things for others and God but not always taking time to bask in His Word for guidance and strength.

The truth is this: we've all felt like this at some point in our lives. We've all had an inkling that there should be more; that there *must* be more to Bible study than reading a verse quickly here and there.

Here's another truth: Jesus waits patiently for us to meet with Him, to seek Him in His Word. He can help us with the distractions that put a wedge between us and Him. It's not about being perfect; it's about surrendering the burdens that weigh down our relationship with God.

He knocks gently on our hearts, hoping we will sense that He's there, waiting (Revelation 3:20). Like eager parents watching their child sleep, looking lovingly at the shape of the child's face and the rise and fall of the chest as the child breathes, Jesus waits patiently for us to wake up to see His face. When you look at someone's face and into their eyes, when you talk to them, you really get to know them.

> The Bible tells us that God says to us, "Seek My face."
> And He wants our response to be, "Your face, Lord,
> I will seek" (Psalm 27:8).

We rarely skip a meal, yet so frequently we skip our spiritual meal. Jesus says, "Seek first the kingdom of God" (Matthew 6:33) and "Give us this day our daily bread" (verse 11), knowing that we need this kind of sustenance more than anything else. Our daily bread is time with God, the very One who sustains us!

Jesus Understands

What encourages me is that Jesus understands what it's like for us, because Satan had a plan to devour Him, too. He watched Jesus for thirty years, looking for His potential weaknesses, carefully crafting a plan to catch Him at His lowest point. One such time was when Jesus was alone and hungry, after being on a spiritual mountaintop at His baptism. Satan heard the words from heaven, "This is My beloved Son, in whom I am well pleased" (Matthew 3:17), and he was determined to make Jesus disbelieve this assurance of His divine mission. "[Jesus] had come to live as a man among men, and it was the word that declared His connection with heaven. It was Satan's purpose to cause Him to doubt that word."[3]

And so, as the Spirit led Jesus into the wilderness, Jesus went to wrestle with what was before Him and to spend time in prayer. "He went to the wilderness to be alone, to contemplate His mission and work. By fasting and prayer He was to brace Himself for the bloodstained path He must travel. But Satan knew that the Savior had gone into the wilderness, and he thought this the best time to approach Him."[4]

I would not have expected Satan to come to Jesus at a time when He was praying to God, but Satan will try to attack and devour us at any time, especially when we're alone. Maybe you've felt this struggle in your life. Maybe you're wrestling with a temptation that seems to be taking over your whole life. Be encouraged and know that Jesus faced what you are facing. And, reading how He dealt with this challenge gives us good guidance.

The three temptations Jesus overcame were highly significant and similar to what you and I face today.

First, the temptation of physical desires such as food, the lust of the flesh, and sensual indulgence. When have you felt the temptation to physically gratify your body? Food, sex, gaming, substances, and so on?

The second temptation was to test whether God was really on Jesus' side. When have you questioned whether God is real? Have you wondered about what's going on in your life and questioned God's involvement?

The third temptation was a test of worship and allegiance. Consider the things that are consuming your time and thoughts at the moment. Have you realized that Satan wants this to be anything but God?

The whispers from the enemy attempt to pierce our thoughts every day: *The Bible is not really relevant to you. It's outdated. The Bible could never help with what you're going through in your life right now. You don't have time for that! Your life is so full already. God is distant and wouldn't be interested in you anyway. Forget it. Don't waste your time.*

These lies of the devil sneak subtly into our minds from time to time, but they couldn't be more false. Ellen White said, "By what means did

---

3. Ellen G. White, *The Desire of Ages* (Oakland, CA: Pacific Press Publishing Association, 1898), 119.

4. White, *The Desire of Ages*, 114. You can also read about this in Matthew 4:1–11; Mark 1:12, 13; and Luke 4:1–13.

[Jesus] overcome in the conflict with Satan? By the word of God. Only by the word could He resist temptation. . . . Every promise in God's word is ours. 'By every word that proceedeth out of the mouth of God' are we to live. When assailed by temptation, look not to circumstances or to the weakness of self, but to the power of the word. All its strength is yours."[5]

When Jesus faced these three temptations, He responded to each one by rebuking Satan with the words of Scripture, and eventually, the devil, the devouring lion, left Him. The evil one will leave you, too, if you follow Jesus' example and use the Bible as your weapon. Ephesians 6:10–17 says,

> Finally, be strong in the Lord and in his mighty power. Put on the full armor of God, so that you can take your stand against the devil's schemes. For our struggle is not against flesh and blood, but against the rulers, against the authorities, against the powers of this dark world and against the spiritual forces of evil in the heavenly realms. Therefore put on the full armor of God, so that when the day of evil comes, you may be able to stand your ground, and after you have done everything, to stand. Stand firm then, with the belt of truth buckled around your waist, with the breastplate of righteousness in place, and with your feet fitted with the readiness that comes from the gospel of peace. In addition to all this, take up the shield of faith, with which you can extinguish all the flaming arrows of the evil one. Take the helmet of salvation and the sword of the Spirit, which is the word of God. (NIV)

We can use God's words, which hold more power than anything else on this earth, to overcome the enemy. It is a sure source of power and hope in this world! God is so much mightier than Satan—and He should be the One we focus on. Don't look at your circumstances or how weak you feel. Look to God. Claim His power in His word. When you are walking with Jesus, all His strength is yours.

---

5. White, *The Desire of Ages*, 123.

3

The Power of the Word

Once God has spoken;
twice have I heard this:
that power belongs to God.
Psalm 62:11, ESV

S ome time ago I went to meetings at a church organization for a day. I joined the morning staff worship before the day began. Someone read from a short devotional to about forty workers who sat in rows. I sat on the end of a row, looking with curiosity at the faces of those around me. I saw various responses. Some looked out the window, seeming eager to get on with the day. Others looked a little blank, perhaps disconnected. Others were listening. I waited, hungry for some takeaway words that would fill me as the day began. Before I knew it, a short prayer was offered and everyone rushed off to start the day.

I found myself longing for more; longing perhaps for what God was waiting to give, and wondering whether others had, too. While I've read many good devotionals, as I'm sure you have too, there's nothing as deep or inspiring as the Bible itself. I wondered what it might look like if a stack of Bibles lived in a corner of that room and whether anything would change if the workers picked one up each morning. I wondered what might happen in the lives of these workers, and in their work, if they read from the Bible each morning, together. If they simply *read together*, perhaps they could reflect and consider how the passage gives guidance to them personally or to their work for the day ahead.

And then, what would happen if they prayed for one another—for their work, their families, their challenges—before they rushed on to their day? What would happen if, instead of trusting the common wisdom of committees in our workplaces, we turned to the inspired advice in the Bible? What would happen if we paused to really seek such advice and then followed it, even if it didn't make worldly sense to us? What would happen?

If you are a leader, how can you turn to God's Word for advice in leading your team? How can you show that the Bible is living, breathing, and powerful in giving guidance today—in your meetings, your everyday work, and in your plans for the future? How can you be more confident to trust God in your work decisions?

If you are a parent, how can you turn to God's Word for advice about how to work with the challenges you face with your children or your spouse? How can you claim the promises in the Bible to change the tone in your home?

If we were to bring the Bible into our lives without hesitation, I believe we would see huge changes in our lives, in our homes, and in our workplaces because God's Word is powerful in so many ways!

The Bible makes this appeal of itself: "Receive, please, instruction from His mouth, and lay up His words in your heart" (Job 22:22). Did you notice the "please" appeal in that sentence? The Bible authors knew how valuable these words are. No other book on earth can speak to your life as these words can.

The words sit there on the pages of your Bible, but how can you keep God's words in your heart? We can start by putting them there in an intentional way. "Your word I have hidden in my heart," David said, "that I might not sin against You" (Psalm 119:11). It means keeping God's words in our hearts, where we have easy access to them.

What else does the Bible say about these words of God's?

God's Words Are Alive and Powerfully Relevant

The Bible is "living and powerful, and sharper than any two-edged sword, piercing even to the division of soul and spirit, and of joints and marrow, and is a discerner of the thoughts and intents of the heart" (Hebrews 4:12). If you've ever seen a two-edged sword, you know how sharp and how powerful it is. For a book to be described like this, it must be extremely awe-inspiring.

The Bible describes itself as being alive. You might be curious as to how this could be since it was written thousands of years ago. Jesus said, "The words that I speak to you are spirit, and they are life" (John 6:63). This verse means that if your heart is broken or your life is falling apart, God can speak His words into your world and change things around. The Old Testament describes these words as being very active and not at all stagnant or passive:

> "So shall My word be that goes forth from My mouth;
> It shall not return to Me void,
> But it shall accomplish what I please,
> And it shall prosper in the thing for which I sent it."
> (Isaiah 55:11)

The words in your Bible have come from God Himself. God sent them specifically for you. When you read them with a prayerful, open heart, they won't be wasted.

David wrote a profound statement when he said that he considered the impact of God's words on his life:

> This is my comfort in my affliction,
> For Your word has given me life. (Psalm 119:50)

God's words can give us life too.

God's Word "Tastes" Good

You may or may not have ever experienced severe hunger. Maybe you've fasted or gone on a diet. After you've felt intense hunger, food tastes so good! In a spiritual sense, the Bible is food for our souls. Maybe your soul is empty and hungry at the moment. Maybe you long for it to be filled with something that is lasting. God's words taste good to the mind and heart:

> Your words were found, and I ate them,
> And Your word was to me the joy and rejoicing of my heart.
> (Jeremiah 15:16)

> "It is written, 'Man shall not live by bread alone, but by every
> word that proceeds from the mouth of God.' " (Matthew 4:4)

As newborn babes, desire the pure milk of the word, that you may grow thereby, if indeed you have tasted that the Lord is gracious. (1 Peter 2:2)

When we read God's words and truly soak them up, they will fill us and sustain us as they promise to.

God's Word Is Pure, Solid Truth

I stood in line at a clothing store, and I noticed some tote bags for sale near the counter. Some said, "Truth is what YOU want," while others said, "Follow your dreams—no one else will." And yet others said, "Your way is the only highway." These subtle messages, ultimately focused on self, speak strongly of a popular culture where truth, success, and one's future are portrayed as relative, changing, and personal.

A trend among some liberal theologians in the 1960s was to write God out of the field of theology. In 2017, a cover story of *Time* magazine featured the headline, "Is Truth Dead?" This trend illustrates the position of our society now. The idea of truth is decaying in society to such an extent that no one knows what truth is anymore. According to popular culture, there is no measuring stick, no foundation that remains constant and can be depended upon to endure the test of time.

Contrary to this worldview, the Bible claims that God is truth and that Jesus and His Word testify about Him. Here are a few examples from the Bible about God's Word as truth:

"Sanctify them by Your truth. Your word is truth." (John 17:17)

When you received the word of God which you heard from us, you welcomed it not as the word of men, but as it is in truth, the word of God, which also effectively works in you who believe. (1 Thessalonians 2:13)

Every word of God is pure;
He is a shield to those who put their trust in Him.
Do not add to His words. (Proverbs 30:5, 6)

The words of the Lord are pure words,
Like silver tried in a furnace of earth,
Purified seven times. (Psalm 12:6)

For the word of the Lord is right,
And all His work is done in truth. (Psalm 33:4, 5)

The Bible declares that truth doesn't change (Matthew 28:18–20). If truth was truth two thousand years ago, it's still truth today. At the same time, as we read God's Word, our understanding of God and truth can grow. Ellen White writes, "Truth is an advancing truth,"[1] for "there are mines of truth yet to be discovered by the earnest seeker."[2] "In every age there is a new development of truth, a message of God to the people of that generation."[3] In speaking of "truth," Ellen White always referred to truth as given by God through His Word. We can search for additional light in the Bible because the Bible never contradicts past truths but, instead, builds on them.

What new truth can you discover about God, yourself, and others by searching the Bible?

God's Word Works in Our Hearts and Changes Us

A few years ago, an acquaintance approached me about something personal. She pulled me aside and confronted me in a very direct way. Even though I wanted to resist her comments and defend myself, I listened, which was not easy to do. She walked away, and I was left alone with my thoughts, upset but reflective. Was there any truth in what she had said? I started justifying myself to myself and reasoning away my behavior.

A few weeks later when I sat down to read my Bible and search my heart, the same message resurfaced. I tried to push it away and again began to justify myself in my mind. Then I stopped. I realized that God was trying to change something in me, and if I wanted to be close to Him, I needed to listen to this rebuke. So I came to God and asked Him to show me deeper truths about myself—through His Word. And He did.

As I read and started to study different passages in my Bible, God spoke to me about different personal challenges I was facing. He cut straight to the point in the chapters I read. I surrendered my selfish pride and my desire to be right in my own eyes. I saw that I needed to change. The Holy Spirit convicted me of how desperately I needed Jesus to lead me. Yes, God's Word cut to the very depth of my soul, to the inmost part where no one else could see. I read about, and felt convicted about,

---

1. Ellen G. White, *Counsels to Writers and Editors* (Nashville, TN: Southern Publishing Association, 1946), 33.
2. Ellen G. White, *Testimonies for the Church*, vol. 5 (Mountain View, CA: Pacific Press Publishing Association, 1948), 704.
3. White, *Christ's Object Lessons*, 127.

changes that needed to happen in my life. Those ancient words, written thousands of years ago, spoke directly to my soul. I knew this wasn't a coincidence.

These words on the page were *alive* and *powerful!* It was as though God were sitting beside me, speaking to me in a way no one else had. God certainly doesn't hold back with His words! He says it as it is, and as we need to hear it, without tiptoeing around our issues. But He also lavishes His extravagant love on us with His words. He delights in us (Psalm 147:10, 11), sings over us (Zephaniah 3:17), will never leave us (Deuteronomy 31:6), wants to sit down and dine with us (Revelation 3:20), and will give us His peace that passes our human understanding (Philippians 4:7).

Wow, what power! What extravagant love. The Holy Spirit leading me to the Bible passages I needed to read is not out of the ordinary. This has happened to me many times, and maybe it's happened to you too.

We must be careful not to expect the Bible to serve our purposes or perspectives, which are not always the same as God's. For example, we shouldn't use the "close my eyes and point to a text" method because this is not how God wants to communicate with us through His Word. The Holy Spirit guides and teaches us as we read. First Corinthians 2:13 says, "These things we also speak, not in words which man's wisdom teaches but which the Holy Spirit teaches, comparing spiritual things with spiritual." Ellen White explains it this way: "God intends that even in this life the truths of His word shall be ever unfolding to His people. There is only one way in which this knowledge can be obtained. We can attain to an understanding of God's word only through the illumination of that Spirit by which the word was given."[4]

When we come to the Bible with a humble spirit and an open heart, the Holy Spirit *will* be there. He will speak straight to our need. His words will change what needs to be changed in our attitude, thoughts, and behavior; they guide us, giving light to the path in front of us, showing how to live our lives. The Bible tells us that there's power in the Word (Hebrews 4:12) and also says, "Receive with meekness the implanted word, which is able to save your souls" (James 1:21).

Ultimately, we must choose what to do with God's words. Like Adam and Eve, we can listen and then try to justify why we should live contrary to them, or by asking the Holy Spirit to guide us as we read, we

---

4. Ellen G. White, *Steps to Christ* (Oakland, CA: Pacific Press Publishing Association, 1892), 109.

can choose to let God's words transform our lives in ways that no other words in this world can. It's up to us to choose what we do with the words on the pages.

Considering what God has done for us changes us; the Word changes everything. These become not just words on a page but living, true words that affect everything in our lives.

God's Word Gives a Double Blessing

Recently I boarded a plane for an international work trip. When I found my seat and got settled, I had an uneasy feeling that the plane would not make it to its destination. I often fly for work and had never had those thoughts before. As I looked at the faces of the passengers around me, I started praying, "God, do you want me to get off this plane? Are these uneasy feelings from You, or not?" I sent a message to Matt, asking him to pray for me.

Then, out of the blue, I received a message from a friend I hadn't heard from for a while. Her message simply said, "Fear not, for I am with you, be not dismayed, for I am your God. I will strengthen you, Yes I will help you, I will uphold you with My righteous right hand" (Isaiah 41:10). Wonder and gratitude filled me as I knew that God was telling me in His amazing way not to worry about this trip, that He would go with me and protect me. What my friend had read that morning had been such a blessing to me because she responded to the Holy Spirit prompting her to share it.

Something striking about the power of God's Word is that when we study His word, often what He shares with us will be used to encourage someone else that the day. Isaiah 50:4 tells us:

"The Lord GOD has given Me
The tongue of the learned,
That I should know how to speak a word in season to him
who is weary.
He awakens Me morning by morning,
He awakens My ear
To hear as the learned."

Our personal Bible study time not only strengthens us but enables us to encourage others we may meet that day. And so our Bible study time becomes a double blessing!

What I love about the verse in Isaiah is that God says He knows we feel weary, yet He wakens us morning by morning, desiring to teach us so that we can speak for Him. I've come to love the invisible nudge of God that wakes me up each morning, before the sun rises, knowing that He wants to spend time with me—that I can also share His messages with others.

When God asks us to share His words of encouragement with others, may our response be,

> "The Lord God has opened My ear
> And I was not rebellious,
> Nor did I turn away." (Isaiah 50:5)

God's Word Speaks of His Heart

While a person's eyes can be a window to their soul, a person's words also tell us a lot about them. The Bible says, "Out of the abundance of the heart . . . the mouth speaks" (Matt. 15:18). When we have junk in our hearts, it comes out in our words.

Like me, you've no doubt experienced feeling frustrated, tired, or stressed and how that state of mind changes what comes out of your mouth—words that we often regret. You may have also experienced the opposite, when your heart is bursting with love for someone and you can't hold back your words!

God's word speaks of His heart and His intentions toward us. They are incredibly powerful, and we have them in our very possession in Scripture. If you think about how God has used His words throughout history, it's incredible to see the power they hold. Take a look at these amazing examples:

- God's word brought the world into existence (Hebrews 11:3; Psalm 33:6).

- Jesus' words and His touch brought sight to the blind (John 9) and hearing to the deaf (Matt. 11:5).

- By Jesus' words, those who know and love Him will be resurrected at the second coming (1 Thessalonians 4:16).

- We can fight the enemy with God's word (Ephesians 6:17).

- God's word can save our souls: "So get rid of all the filth and evil in your lives, and humbly accept the word God has planted in your hearts, for it has the power to save your souls" (James 1:21, NLT).

God tells us, "Lay up these words of mine in your heart and in your soul, and bind them as a sign on your hand, and they shall be as frontlets between your eyes" (Deuteronomy 11:18). These are powerful words that, when we think and act on them, can radically change our lives. These words from God's heart are given to us so "that He might make you know that man shall not live by bread alone; but man lives by every word that proceeds from the mouth of the LORD" (Deuteronomy 8:3). These are extraordinary words that we need to really live!

God's Word Will Lead You to Jesus Christ

While Jesus was on this earth, He showed us what God was like in the flesh (John 14:9). Since we didn't meet Jesus while He was on earth, God's Word, the Bible, is the clearest picture of Jesus we have available to us.

The Bible is not a mystery to be deciphered or an outdated book that holds no relevance. Rather, it is like a love letter or like a long text message from God. The Bible will give you wisdom and knowledge about many different things, but in particular, when you read it with an open heart, the Holy Spirit will bring you into a relationship with Jesus Christ.

No matter what Bible passage or story I read, I can see Jesus when I look for Him because He desires to draw me to Himself: "Yes, I have loved you with an everlasting love; therefore with lovingkindness I have drawn you" (Jeremiah 31:3, NKJV).

The Bible is about the God who has such intense love for us that He does all He can to woo us to Him. You simply must open the Bible for yourself to discover this incredible God who wants you to know Him for yourself.

Finally, God's Word Will Stand Forever

Our character and our relationships will be the things that endure forever. In this same way, God's Word won't change or disappear but will stand throughout eternity. The Bible says of itself:

"The grass withers, the flower fades,
But the word of God stands forever." (Isaiah 40:8)

Forever, O LORD,
Your word is settled in heaven.
Your faithfulness endures to all generations. (Psalm 119:89)

Consider how few things will endure forever. Surely this Book is something we should consider!

"There is nothing more calculated to strengthen the intellect than the study of the Scriptures. No other book is so potent to elevate the thoughts, to give vigor to the faculties, as the broad, ennobling truths of the Bible. If God's word were studied as it should be, men would have a breadth of mind, a nobility of character, and a stability of purpose rarely seen in these times."[5]

Before you continue reading, I invite you to reflect for a moment on this question: How is God's Word positioned in your life right now?

---

5. White, *Steps to Christ*, 90.

4

Approaching the Word

I sat in a Bible study small group, listening with interest. We'd just read Leviticus 25–27 about the Jubilee concept of land being returned to the owners after seven years. As we discussed these chapters, I could hear two contrasting views coming from two friends. Max was convicted that all we own belongs to God, that He blesses us with "land" and that we should return everything to Him when we covenant with Him. In contrast, Sarah said she believed that this story was simply a record in the history of what happened to the land at that time.

How is it that when two people read the same Bible passage, they can sometimes glean different things from it? And how is it that when I read a Bible passage today, my takeaway can be different from a thought that affected me two years earlier?

You may have heard stories about people who had never heard about God but read the Bible and were changed forever. You may have also heard about people who have read the Bible many times but still don't believe that God exists.

The State of My Heart

In Jesus' day, the Pharisees were the elite of society. They were rigorously trained to the point that by the time they were ten years old, they had memorized the entire Torah (first five books of the Bible), and by the time they were fourteen, many had memorized the majority of the Hebrew Bible (the Old Testament). Impressive! Yet, despite the fact that they could quote large portions of Scripture, when they met God's Son Jesus face-to-face, they didn't recognize Him. Their biases and personal expectations stood in the way. It's interesting to read what the Bible thinks of this: "But the natural man does not receive the things of the Spirit of God, for they are foolishness to him; nor can he know them, because they are *spiritually discerned*" (1 Corinthians 2:14, emphasis added).

What does it mean to be spiritually discerning, and how can we be spiritually discerning when we read the Bible? The *Merriam-Webster* dictionary defines *discerning* as "showing insight and understanding."[1] In light of this, to have spiritual insight and understanding is what we need when it comes to the Bible. If I think the Bible is foolish, then I'm not going to be looking for truth in its pages. So it seems that both my attitude and the way I approach reading the Bible are *very* important.

A spiritually open-minded person will have very different takeaways compared to those of a closed-minded person. Paul says it this way: "When you received the word of God, which you heard from us, you accepted it not as a human word, but as it actually is, the word of God, which is indeed at work in you who believe" (1 Thessalonians 2:13, NIV). God's Word works in us when we believe. Isn't this an amazing concept? When I open my Bible and believe that God has something to say to me through the words on the pages, He will indeed speak to me and work in my life. But so much of that depends on my faith and my expectations.

And so it seems that the ball sits largely in our court. We can believe that the Bible is God's Word and approach it as such, or we can see it as just another narrative history book that shares interesting stories. Our attitude and approach to the Bible will make a difference in what we take away from it.

---

1. *Merriam-Webster*, s.v. "discerning," accessed August 6, 2018, https://www.merriam-webster.com/dictionary/discerning.

The good news is that when we don't believe, God can and will help us. We can say, like the troubled father who met Jesus, "Lord, I believe, help my unbelief!" (Mark 9:24). Indeed, without God's help, we could not even desire anything of God in the first place. It's not merely up to us (this would be too difficult!), but God seeks us every day, and He helps us to say "Yes!" to what He is already doing in us (Philippians 2:12, 13). How we approach God's Word—the spirit in our hearts (our underlying belief in the Bible, or lack of it)—will certainly affect what we take away from our reading. "The spirit in which you come to the investigation of the Scriptures will determine the character of the assistant at your side. Angels from the world of light will be with those who in humility of heart seek for divine guidance. But if the Bible is opened with irreverence, with a feeling of self-sufficiency, if the heart is filled with prejudice, Satan is beside you, and he will set the plain statements of God's word in a perverted light."[2]

In contrast, "as we try to become acquainted with our heavenly Father through His word, angels will draw near, our minds will be strengthened, our characters will be elevated and refined. We shall become more like our Saviour."[3] If we open our Bibles in humility and prayer, God will speak to us.

Sometimes biblical knowledge confronts something in our lives and makes us feel uncomfortable (like a particular sin we are struggling with, as I mentioned in the previous chapter). So when I read the timeless words in the pages of my Bible, the question is, Is my heart open to what God is speaking into my life? Whether it's about my lack of time for Him, my selfish ways, my apathy to abiding in Him—whatever it is, the Bible calls me to account.

I believe one purpose of the Bible is to speak truth into my life about my status with God and how to improve this relationship. If my heart is open to the Holy Spirit working in my life, if I approach the Word with humility, I will always come away changed. But if I hold on to my apathy and my sin, I will read it to prove the text wrong so that I don't have to change.

And so, as we read the Bible, we should constantly ask ourselves: What state of heart and mind am I in as I approach the Bible? Am I seeing the message before me in the context of the whole Bible? Am I bringing my

2. Ellen G. White, *Gospel Workers* (Battle Creek, MI: Review and Herald Publishing Association, 1892), 127.

3. White, *The Desire of Ages*, 70.

opinions to the Bible when I read, with the goal of trying to justify my thoughts, or am I coming with an open mind and heart, ready to see what God wants to tell me today, with childlike faith?

> We should exert all the powers of the mind in the study of the Scriptures and should task the understanding to comprehend, as far as mortals can, the deep things of God; yet we must not forget that the docility and submission of a child is the true spirit of the learner. . . . We should not engage in the study of the Bible with that self-reliance with which so many enter the domains of science, but with a prayerful dependence upon God and a sincere desire to learn His will. We must come with a humble and teachable spirit to obtain knowledge from the great I AM. Otherwise, evil angels will so blind our minds and harden our hearts that we shall not be impressed by the truth.[4]

God waits to speak to us, to change us and mold us to abide in Him. The Holy Spirit waits to move us closer to Jesus Christ. Do we want to step closer? Are we ready to surrender? If we are, we will become "wise unto salvation," and we'll see things we never even imagined! God will speak directly to our concerns, our questions, our needs, and our joys. We will experience firsthand that the Bible is "living and powerful" (Hebrews 4:12).

It's also important to see the Bible as a whole package rather than picking and choosing the parts that feel comfortable to us. It can be easy to read the familiar, easy passages and leave out the confronting ones. If we truly want God to speak into our lives, we must take the Bible as a whole, trusting that God will reveal what we need, when we need it.

Martin Luther puts it this way: "For a number of years I have now annually read through the Bible twice. If the Bible were a large, mighty tree and all its words were little branches, I would have tapped at all the branches, eager to know what was there and what it had to offer."[5]

Scripture, the Authority

The role of human reason is a huge topic that I'm not going to explore in much depth here, except to say that God does not ignore or bypass human reason.

---

4. White, *The Great Controversy*, 599.
5. Martin Luther, *What Luther Says: An Anthology*, vol. 1, comp. Ewald M. Plass (Saint Louis, MO: Concordia Publishing House, 1959), 83.

He created human beings in His image and invites us to dialogue with Him. We can see this happening in many biblical narratives where God has discussions with humans such as Enoch, Abraham, Moses, and Job. In the Gospels we have a record of many conversations Jesus had with people. It would be fair to say that God doesn't bypass human reason but invites us to learn to work within His large, infinite patterns of reason, even inviting us to "reason together" (Isaiah 1:18) when working out our salvation and other important topics.

In our relationship with God, the Author of Scripture, we can't ignore our mind, but God asks us to inform our minds of His vast reaches of knowledge and understanding through His Book.

I think back to when I was a student in high school, studying for my final math exam. It seemed like the hardest thing in the world before I started studying because it wasn't my natural ability—or my joy! But through persistence and study, I eventually had clarity and was prepared for that exam. In a similar way, certain chapters in the Bible may seem overwhelming, but I've found that through prayer, tenacity in study, asking for the Holy Spirit's help, plus many times comparing one part of Scripture with another part and discussing things with others, the biblical concepts become clear.

Jesus urged us, "Love the LORD your God with all your heart, with all your soul, and with all your mind" (Matthew 22:37), and I believe that He doesn't expect us to bypass the intellect He has given us when we do that. Rather, we're invited to study, learn, and discover the vast parameters of divine reasoning found in Scripture.

However, it is possible for human reason to leave God out of the picture (consciously or unconsciously), and when we do, we try to work things out on our own, placing self as equal to or above God in our thinking. It's not unusual for people to approach Scripture with an air of confidence, when we believe we've heard it all before or when we think we understand all there is to know. It's usually when we feel important, confident, self-sufficient, and in need of nothing that we neglect our relationship with God and rely on our own knowledge and reasoning.

But God is God, and we are not God. Our tendency to feel pride in our abilities and human thought (which are all God-given in the first place) shouldn't get in the way of our relying on the Creator of the universe—the One who was there from the beginning of time and inspired the writing of His book. "Can anyone teach God knowledge, since He judges those on high?" (Job 21:22).

Don't think that you have to be super smart to really understand the Bible. God gave His Word for everyone to know Him more. Everyone! That is you and me, not just the theologians. It is true that the value of the rich, deep insights offered through the work of those who dig deeply into the original languages and theology of the Bible cannot be underestimated. The fact remains, however, that when we read the Bible with an open, prayerful heart, God speaks plainly to us through His Word.

The Bible is the source of truth on this earth that has remained unchanged throughout time. Jesus is the same yesterday, today, and forever—as is His Word (Hebrews 13:8). The same God who created and guided His people, who loved so intensely that He sent Jesus to save us from ourselves, this same God wants to speak to you through His timeless Word today. His message is still the same: "Come close to Me. I will give your souls rest. I will take your burdens, bind up your brokenness, give you guidance for your life. I will give you peace" (see Matthew 11:28; Jeremiah 29:11). Why do we try to go it alone with such an offer on hand? It's the fallen-human inclination to be independent, to say, "Thanks, God. I've got this. I don't need You or Your guidance in my life."

For some in ages past, to claim that the Bible is God's truth has taken courage. Many people have died rather than give up their faith in God and His Word. People still die for this conviction, even today. Perhaps it takes a serious kind of boldness for you or me to follow God's Word. Consider this strong statement:

> It is one thing to treat the Bible as a book of good moral instruction, to be heeded so far as it is consistent with the spirit of the times and our position in the world; it is another thing to regard it as it really is—the word of the living God, the word that is our life, the word that is to mold our actions, our words, and our thoughts. To hold God's word as anything less than this is to reject it. And this rejection by those who profess to believe it, is foremost among the causes of skepticism and infidelity in the youth.[6]

As Creator, God has made everything, which He said was very good. And yet, despite the beauty in the heavens and on earth, and anything

---

6. Ellen G. White, *Education* (Oakland, CA: Pacific Press Publishing Association, 1903), 260.

humans build or create, there is one thing that gets God's attention. Do you know what it is? He tells us in Isaiah 66:2:

> "But on this one will I look:
> On him who is poor and of a contrite spirit,
> And who trembles at My word."

Do we come to the Bible in humility, knowing we don't know it all and being open to God revealing truth to us? Do we respect His Word? If so, you have God's attention more than anything else on earth.

5

Lingering Light: God and You

"Your words were found, and I ate them, and your words
became to me a joy and the delight of my heart."
Jeremiah 15:16

My First Bible

At Christmastime when I was six years old, all of our extended family from my dad's side had come together, and all thirteen of us were staying in a small house at The Entrance, a beautiful beach in New South Wales, Australia. We loved getting together for Christmas every second year, and that year was one that I'll never forget.

My dear Russian grandmother, my Babie (short for Babushka), was unwell, although we didn't know it at the time. She had a brain tumor that eventually took her life, and this ended up being our last Christmas together. It brings tears to my eyes even now as I remember her most loving and gentle eyes, which looked into your very soul, and her utter selfless and beautiful character and deep love for Jesus.

For Christmas, Babie gave each of the four of us oldest cousins a picture Bible. When I first opened it, I saw the striking red front cover and read the words "The Picture Bible" in gold foil. Then I opened the pages and saw all the amazing, colorful pictures inside, and my mind boggled in wonder.

I vividly remember my grandmother telling the four of us, "This is a very special book, the most special book you'll ever own. It's a Bible. You must treat it with great respect because it's God's book. Be sure never to put anything on top of it. And most of all, remember this: God loves you so much that He wants you to read His words to you."

I remember holding that Bible in my six-year-old hands and looking at it with great awe. God loves me *that* much that He's written to *me*? It seemed too amazing to be true.

I also remember what one of my cousins and I did that afternoon. We took a small table from inside the house and placed it outside under a tree on the back lawn. We found a pretty tablecloth, and on it, we respectfully placed our new Bibles. They sat there in the shade while we played in the yard. Now and then I would look over to make sure my Bible was still there, feeling a sense of childlike amazement that God had given me His words and that my grandmother loved me so much that she would give me the best present ever that Christmas.

I loved reading that picture Bible over the years that followed. I pondered the pictures for hours. And as I read the words, I could almost hear God's voice speaking to me. I still have this Bible in my bookcase.

A few years later, my parents gave me my first "grown-up" Bible, and I loved watching my mum show me how and why she had highlighted her Bible before I started to personalize my new one from her. But I'll never forget the deep impression and sense of awe that first red Bible had on me as a child and how I knew God had spoken to me through that Bible in ways it's hard to describe.

If you're a parent with young children, consider how you will give your child their first Bible. Make it a special, memorable event. Perhaps you could write a personal message inside the front cover, wrap it beautifully, and place it at the end of their bed as a surprise one morning. Or you could have a special evening worship planned (perhaps a Friday night) and could show your child your Bible and talk about how it has encouraged and helped you in your life before giving one to your child. However you choose to give your child a Bible, if you create a memorable event around the importance of this incredible book, it will linger with them forever, as it has with me.

Thirsty but Not Drinking

We've identified that the devil does all he can to keep us away from God's Word to weaken us. We've also looked at the importance of coming to the Bible with a humble, open mind and heart. One of the most surprising things I have realized lately is just how many Christians wish they read their Bibles more. In fact, according to a Barna survey, 62 percent of Americans identify with this sentiment.[1] At times I've struggled to be consistent with Bible study and have thought that there must be an easier way. I've wondered:

Where do I start?
What's the difference between reading and studying my Bible?
Surely it can't be this hard, so why does it feel so hard?

Perhaps you have tried to read the Bible through in a year. Maybe you've given up after a few weeks of hurriedly reading one or two chapters a day because it felt like just another thing to check off your daily list. Perhaps you've struggled because the words sometimes feel empty, and it seemed as though they *could* reach into your life but didn't always do so, and you wondered why.

Sometimes I've looked at the clock and thought, *Right. I have fifteen minutes before I need to shower, eat breakfast, and get to work. I need to be efficient in these things. I've got fifteen minutes to read and pray—I'll get to it!* I've gone through the motions very quickly and at the end of my fifteen minutes felt unsatisfied but continued the rush into my day, only a little satisfied that I've appeased my conscience and spent fifteen minutes reading my Bible.

Then I come across statements like this, which stop me in my tracks: "There is but little benefit derived from a hasty reading of the Scriptures. One may read the whole Bible through and yet fail to see its beauty or comprehend its deep and hidden meaning."[2]

I know this to be true. My hasty reading has given me little benefit. *The reason I read my Bible is not to know my Bible more but to know God more (and in the process, myself).* If the Bible is the main way God communicates with me, how can I expect Him to do so when I don't pause long enough to let Him?

Yes, we're busy people in a rushed society, and I believe this is a key reason why so many thirst for more from the Word of God but just aren't drinking. Instead of finding joy in our reading, it can sometimes feel like a burden we need to meet—of, say, a chapter per day. If we don't "keep

---

1. "The State of the Bible: 6 Trends for 2014," Barna Group, April 8, 2014, https://www.barna.com/research/the-state-of-the-bible-6-trends-for-2014/.

2. White, *Steps to Christ*, 90.

up" with what we think we should be reading, guilt can drive us away from spending time with God.

R. C. Sproul challenges me when he says, "Here, then, is the real problem of our negligence. We fail in our duty to study God's Word not so much because it is difficult to understand, not so much because it is dull and boring, but because it is work. Our problem is not a lack of intelligence or a lack of passion. Our problem is that we are lazy."[3]

Ouch. Maybe I am lazy. It's true that it takes work and a commitment. If I read my Bible only when I feel like it, I would probably rarely read it! There will always be other distractions that take the place of time to read my Bible.

Imagine a man walking through a wilderness. This man has been walking for a long time without stopping. His journey isn't easy, and he is desperately thirsty. He finally finds a stream, and is overcome with joy! He rushes to the bank, kneels down, and starts to drink. As he's drinking, he doesn't stop to ask himself, "What is the least amount I can drink to satisfy my thirst?" No! Instead, he asks, "How deeply can I drink this water?"[4]

In the same way, I imagine that it must break God's heart to see us wondering how little we can read of His words. In Jeremiah 17:8 we read about a tree that is planted by water. This tree has roots in the stream, so it doesn't need to fear when heat or drought comes. This tree represents us. When we choose to be planted beside the cool water of God's Word, and when we start to drink, really drink, we realize just how thirsty we are, and drinking no longer seems like a chore but the greatest thing on earth.

Finding Time

Making time to read your Bible may be one of your greatest challenges. I've heard people talk about how wonderful it is to spend time with God every morning, so I've tried to do so too. Over the years I've struggled to wake up to study my Bible. Because of work commitments, I've become a night person, and I would hear about people waking up early to study their Bible and thought that wasn't possible for me. If I wanted to

---

3. R. C. Sproul, *Knowing Scripture*, 2nd ed. (Downers Grove, IL: InterVarsity Press, 2009), 20.

4. Jeremy Adelman, "Do You Read the Bible Enough? desiringGod, Oct. 27, 2016, https://www.desiringgod.org/articles/do-you-read-the-bible-enough.

read my Bible, I would set my alarm and drag myself out of bed fifteen minutes earlier than usual to do so, and I would spend the majority of my time trying to wake up before I scanned a chapter of the Bible, then went on my way.

Perhaps you've done this too, and if so, I understand how you feel. I think God also understands, and I encourage you to talk to Him about it. Something happened to me a few years ago when I truly surrendered my time to God. I asked Him to wake me up in the mornings. It wasn't a passing request but a heartfelt cry that was like this: "God, *please* help me to desire You. I *know* I need to spend time with You, and I *want* to love Your Word. I know You can speak to me through it. But I need You to help me. Please wake me up with enough time to spend with You. You know my life is way too full already, but I can't do this without You any longer. And Lord, can you help me not to feel so tired?"

After I prayed this prayer, I started to wake up early, without an alarm, usually before five o'clock in the morning. I would be in the deepest sleep and all of a sudden wake up. I knew God had answered my prayer. Of course, He was eager and waiting to spend time with me! When this happened day after day, I found myself in a routine and met with God downstairs in a cozy corner in my office. As the days and months went by, I expected to feel tired, but surprisingly, I wasn't. Instead of reaching for my phone to see whether any emails had arrived overnight, I made a commitment to spend time with God first, before anything else. That personal challenge isn't always easy, and I am often tempted to launch into other things. But if I have chosen God to be number one in my life, surely I can honor Him as my priority every morning.

Jesus gave us this example: "Now in the morning, having risen a long while before daylight, He went out and departed to a solitary place; and there He prayed" (Mark 1:35). Imagine with me for a moment, Jesus, seemingly alone to the onlooker but abiding with God, sitting by the Sea of Galilee or on the side of a hill, praying and communing with His Father before the world around Him woke up. I'm sure this time was what gave Him strength to face all that He faced while being separated from His Father. If Jesus needed this time each day, how much more do we?

Being with God while the world around me sleeps ensures that I have uninterrupted time with Him. The world seems quieter, my mind alert but still, when I come to God in the early hours of the morning. There is no doubt that it's a different kind of Bible study if, instead, I come to the Word mid-morning. The phone may ring; there are distractions outside. Inside my heart, I'm already started with the day and less inclined to linger with the Lord. But in the stillness of the early hours of the morning, I come to Him in solitude and peace, before the business of the day awakens the world. God waits for me every morning.

I've come to realize that when I respond to God's call to spend time with Him, He gives me more energy for the day ahead than if I sleep in. At times (especially in winter) it's hard to move from under those warm blankets, but when God wakes me up, I can't resist spending time with Him. Before I swing my legs over the side of my bed, I ask Him to bless our time together and to give me an alert mind and a receptive heart. As light lingers in the early hours of each morning, having that time with God has become the most valuable time of my day—hands down.

If you're stretched and crazy-busy, pray that God will help you. I believe that more than anything, He wants to spend time with you—time away from your busy schedule. Time away from the rush and noise of each day. The early hours of the morning, as the sun rises outside and the warmth of His Word flows into your life, will become precious to you. You'll bask in the words that direct your life, these words that give you courage and wisdom and peace to face whatever surrounds you that day. This time with God will affect your day as nothing else will, and will give you great strength.

There's a saying: "If you do what you always did, you'll get what you always got." Similarly, if you fail to plan, you plan to fail. These sayings are also true of Bible study, which is why it's good to have some options for when and how to study your Bible. You may have heard how others study their Bibles, or maybe you've even had someone give you a Bible study before. It's good to have some ideas, and I'll be sharing some with you in the following chapter. You will start to navigate a study plan yourself, and this time will become very meaningful as you grow in your relationship with God.

I regularly make a covenant with God. I ask Him to help me keep that daily appointment with Him. He wants to spend time with me—and with you!—more than we can imagine. I think about Him standing patiently at the door of my heart, knocking gently, waiting to spend time with me (Revelation 3:20).

I've also realized that I shouldn't rush my time with God. Life seems so rushed, and I don't want to quickly pass over reading God's words. There's no need to multitask here, when the best thing for my soul is to let God, the true Light of the world, speak into my life (John 1:9). When we give Him our first, best time (for me, the mornings), our lives radically change.

Finally, if you miss your time with God some mornings, don't give up. Sometimes an emergency arises, or for some reason, you're just not able to meet with God. I never feel as grounded on those days, and I find myself missing the one-on-one communion with God through His Word. But it doesn't stop me from abiding in Him later in the day, or again the next morning. It's certainly not something God would want us to feel bad about or a reason for us not to pick up where we left off. However, don't let too many days, weeks, or months pass without daily spending time with God. Remember that having an abiding relationship with God is a daily decision—and one that you can start today if you choose to.

I challenge you to ask God to wake you up tomorrow so that you can spend time with Him in Bible study and prayer. He will, and He'll also give you the energy you need to get through your day. You'll be amazed at the difference it makes to your day and your relationships when you linger with Him.

Reading or Studying?

Something I've come to realize is that there is a difference between reading and deeply studying (or "basking in") the Bible. Understanding and identifying this difference has completely changed how I spend my time with God in the mornings. I believe the main difference between merely reading the Bible and studying it comes down to one key act: *writing*. It's difficult to study the Bible in our heads. Writing helps us slow down our thoughts, reflect on God's Word, and work through it at a pace where observation, interpretation, application, and commitment can occur. When I choose to pause long enough to put my thoughts onto paper, my initial scattered ideas work themselves out—from my head to my pen and then into my heart and my day. If I don't write down my thoughts, the business of my day swallows me up and I quickly forget what I've studied. I also won't have it as a reference point later.

When I just read the Bible, I usually do so quickly, depending on what else is pressing in my life on that day. If I simply read, I think about the words for a short time and often feel rushed to get on with my day. But if I write something about the words I've read, or even write the words themselves, I am much more likely to remember and take that message with me throughout my day. We are much more likely to remember something we have read when we write a response to it. That's why we write to-do lists and memos—so that we don't forget things! It's similar with the Bible. Writing allows us to savor the taste of God's Word and allows it to linger in our lives throughout the day.

Someone once said, "Reading the Bible without meditating on it is like trying to eat without swallowing." I see writing as part of the "swallowing," or the contemplating. Psalm 119:15, 16 says it this way:

> I will meditate on Your precepts,
> And contemplate Your ways.
> I will delight myself in Your statutes;
> I will not forget Your word.

However, if you're unable to write for some reason, I encourage you to still use the ideas shared in this book. Instead of writing, read aloud the Bible promises and then speak aloud your response to God. There is something so strikingly beautiful about reading the Bible aloud to God and then speaking back to Him what is on your mind and in your heart. This conversation is sure to bless you and draw you near to His heart as you search for jewels in Scripture.

What Things Do I Need When Basking in the Bible?

You have a copy, no doubt, of the most published book in the world. Maybe you have more than one. Maybe it sits by your bed or on your bookshelf. Maybe its pages are worn, underlined and prayed over, or maybe it sits unopened. Either way, you should know this. You don't have to be a theologian to understand the Bible. All you have to do is open it and seek Him with an open heart, and you *will* find Him (Jeremiah 29:13).

You might already have a Bible, but I encourage you to find a Bible with large margins on each side of the page that you can write on. God's word is living and active, and God speaks straight to you and to me through His word (Hebrews 4:12). I believe He wants to interact with us through His living Word, so if you feel comfortable doing it, you may want to write in your Bible. I have many notes all over my Bible, and often when I'm reading a passage I will look at the thoughts or responses I've written in the margins in times past, and it brings the text alive for me in a very personal way.

You will find many, many Bible translations to choose from. Depending on how you want to study, I would recommend something like the New King James Version (NKJV) or English Standard Version (ESV) for a traditional, direct translation, as well as an easy-to-read indirect translation, such as the New Living Translation (NLT). Some Bibles such as *The Living Bible* and *The Clear Word* are paraphrases, which is someone's rewording of the Hebrew and Greek text in their own words. While a paraphrase may help you to see the text in a new or different way, the wording may not help you to understand exactly what is meant and therefore should not be exclusively relied on for study. If you are reading a passage and can read more than one translation, your understanding will be very rich indeed. I do have one Bible (mine is a NKJV study Bible) to use as my main Bible, with all my handwritten notes in it.

If you are looking to buy a Bible for a child, you can buy them an age-appropriate children's Bible. My favorite is *The Illustrated Bible* (New American Standard Bible [NASB]). This is the most beautiful children's Bible I've seen. Every few pages, there are painted pictures that bring the stories to life, so it will keep your child (and you) engaged.

You will also need a journal. There are many nice journals available, either lined or unlined. I also have a colored pencil that I use to highlight Bible promises that are particularly meaningful to me, and a fine-tip pen for writing in the margins of my Bible and in my journal.

Once you have your Bible, a journal or notebook, and a pen, find a quiet place that can be your study spot each day. Some people choose a chair, a corner in a room, or even the floor of a closet. It doesn't matter where you choose, and of course, you can study your Bible anywhere, at any time. I like having a consistent place for the sake of having a daily routine. It will help you to be able to commit to meeting with God each day if you arrange the "date" (which includes the place).

I have a place that I go to each morning to be with God. It used to be in my office, but I've recently moved my study place to the living room because my children often join me in studying their Bibles when they wake up.

School or Work Journal

In addition to my Bible study journal, I have a work journal. Each day I try to write a one-sentence takeaway in this work journal—something that I want to carry with me throughout the day as a reminder of my time with God. It can be a personal challenge, a prayer, or a promise, but by writing it in my work journal, I have something that remains before me throughout the day and has proven to be a great encouragement.

If you're at school, the one-sentence promise or prayer can be a great inspiration, even if you only read it between classes to be encouraged by what God has spoken to you from His Word for that day.

Sometimes it's amazing how personal and pertinent a message can be—a message that I wrote not knowing its significance until later in the day. It's also amazing to look back over past weeks and months and see how God has so clearly spoken about specific issues or prepared me for what is to come through His word.

The Importance of Prayer

It's impossible to overstate the importance of prayer as bookends to (and bookmarks throughout) your Bible study. Ellen White tells us that when we come to read the Bible, we are not alone. By inviting the Holy Spirit to be our guide, we reject all other distractions, and the enemy flees. She says, "The Bible should never be studied without prayer. The Holy Spirit alone can cause us to feel the importance of those things easy to be understood, or prevent us from wresting truths difficult of comprehension."[5] "And Jesus will see us also in the secret places of prayer if we will seek Him for light that we may know what is truth. Angels from the world of light will be with those who in humility of heart seek for divine guidance."[6] "It is the office of heavenly angels to prepare the heart to so comprehend God's word that we shall be charmed with its beauty, admonished by its warnings, or animated and strengthened by its promises."[7] We can hastily ask God to bless us as we read the Bible, or we can pause to surrender our all before we read and invite the Holy Spirit to lead us to a message that we need to hear for that day. This surrender means putting aside our agendas, laying down our will and desires, and being ready to hear the personal daily message that God wants to speak into our lives through His words that morning. More

5. White, *The Great Controversy*, 599, 600.

6. White, *Steps to Christ*, 91.

7. Ellen G. White, *The Spirit of Prophecy*, vol. 4 (Battle Creek, MI: Seventh-day Adventist Publishing Association, 1884), 418.

than anything, it means being humble, completely humble, before the Lord (Psalm 51:17).

Although we talked about this before, I want to emphasize again that whenever I come to study the Bible in a hasty or proud spirit, I finish reading with an attitude of "So what?" and move on with my day. I've come to realize the great importance of a humble spirit, an open heart, and my desire to be with God in my Bible study time. Have no doubt: God will speak through His Word to you, and it will usually be in ways you do not expect, concerning areas of your life you do not expect.

There is power in God's Word, and when we spend time with Him in His Word and invite Him to draw near, He does—and it changes everything. The words on a page become part of a conversation with the God of the universe and will flow into every corner of our lives. Always be grounded in the Bible as your surest source of God's speaking and leading in your life, and beware of other methods of "hearing" God that are not grounded in Scripture.

And don't forget to pray. Praise God for who He is and what He's doing in your life; lay your worries down before Him; seek His advice on questions you have; and ask Him to point out any offensive way in you as you spend time with Him (Psalm 139:24). And then open His Word and listen to Him speak to you through it.

6

Ways to Study Your Bible

You search the Scriptures because you think they give you eternal life.
But the Scriptures point to me!
John 5:39, NLT

Ithink of my sweet friend (whom I mentioned at the beginning of the book) who honestly shared that she didn't know where to start when it came to studying her Bible. And I wonder, how many of us feel the same way but aren't brave enough to declare this? How many of us know that the Bible is a good book to read, but we don't know how to "bask"? And truthfully, we don't have a desire to "linger" in it, either, perhaps because we're too busy and we don't realize how radically it will change our lives.

I'll share some simple ways I bask in God's Word, but before doing so, I want to share that as a Christian mother, I want my children to know Jesus and to know how to know Him deeply through reading His Word. I must say that over the years, I've been at a bit of a loss as to how to instill a desire in my children to want to study and also how to help them study their Bibles. Recently I read this quote that struck me to my heart: "It is because so many parents and teachers profess to believe the word of God while their lives deny its power, that the teaching of Scripture has no greater effect upon the youth. At times the youth are brought to feel the power of the word. They see the preciousness of the love of Christ. They see the beauty of His character, the possibilities of a life given to His service. But in contrast they see the life of those who profess to revere God's precepts."[1] Of course! My own life needs to testify of how the Word of God transforms me in the everyday moments before I can even begin to hope that my children might know it!

As I've spoken to parents of young children, I discovered that my personal experience is not uncommon. I've met very few Christian parents who purposefully teach their children how to study the Bible for themselves. Committed Christian parents often have morning and evening family worship, and they share stories and principles from the Bible, which is a wonderful foundation for the spiritual growth of young children. We know the importance of this from Deuteronomy 6:7–9: "You shall teach them diligently to your children, and shall talk of them when you sit in your house, when you walk by the way, when you lie down, and when you rise up. You shall bind them as a sign on your hand, and they shall be as frontlets between your eyes. You shall write them on the doorposts of your house and on your gates." We have only a few short years to share the Bible with our children while they are young, and God's Word should be infused into our daily lives. We need to be intentional about when and how we do this. God's Word should affect our actions ("a sign on your hand") and our thoughts ("they shall be as frontlets between your eyes"). Our very homes should show physical evidence that we choose whom we are serving.

I was interested to see the results of Barna's American Culture and Faith Institute 2017 survey that revealed that 58 to 70 percent of parents see value in exposing their children to extended family gatherings, church services, art exhibitions, and the Bible, but children spend an average of only two hours per week on these activities. In contrast, 33 to 43 percent of parents do not see value in exposing their children to professional sports, television news, online content, and current movies, yet children spend, on average, seven hours per day on these and related activities.[2]

Barna also showed that statistically, a very small number of younger people have what's called a "biblical worldview" (seeing life through the guidance the Bible gives): only 4 percent of eighteen- to thirty-year-olds and 7 percent of thirty- to forty-nine-year-olds.[3] This confronting statistic reveals the lack of intention about transmitting biblical values to children.

---

1. White, *Education*, 259.

2. Costin Jordache, "George Barna Tells Adventist Delegates, 'We Are in a Crisis,' " *Adventist Review*, May 17, 2017, https://www.adventistreview.org/church-news/story5101-george-barna-tells-adventist-delegates-we-are-in-a-crisis.

3. Jordache, "George Barna."

While it's not always easy for us, Matt and I ensure that worship is a nonnegotiable part of our family's day. We have set times in the morning and evening when we meet in the living room and share meaningful worship as part of our daily routine. We've seen changes in our attitudes, interactions, and how we live together under the same roof as a result of this worship time together. What we do at this time varies and is sometimes led by our children. We read, pray, sometimes sing (especially on Friday nights), and all of us share how God is involved in our daily lives on a personal and practical level.

It's a very meaningful time. However, Matt and I have also started to realize the importance of teaching our children how to study the Bible alone for themselves. Perhaps our sense of urgency comes from seeing how eager children are to learn and spend time with their parents, but also seeing how, over a seemingly quick period, these same children grow up into teenagers and these teachable moments become more and more rare.

So, we've been intentional about showing our three kids, who, as I write this, are eight, ten, and twelve, how to study their Bibles, and I'd love to share a few things we've observed, and some simple strategies that have worked for us. Also, let me share some practical ways that you can dig deeper into God's word in a meaningful way if you are a teenager or an adult of any age.

These Bible study methods are not limited to any age or stage of spiritual growth. The first method is particularly helpful for younger children or anyone who wants to keep things simple. I often use this method myself.

1. Verse-by-Verse Method

As soon as a child learns to read, you can teach them to study their Bible. One of my favorite methods for someone of any age (including me) is the verse-by-verse method. I would recommend this method in particular for young children (six to nine years old) who are learning to read and write. I value the advice of the following statement, which has helped guide me in creating a few simple steps to follow in the verse-by-verse method:

> The study of the Bible demands our most diligent effort and persevering thought. As the miner digs for the golden treasure in the earth, so earnestly, persistently, must we seek for the treasure of God's word.

In daily study the verse-by-verse method is often the most helpful. Let the student take one verse, and concentrate the mind on ascertaining the thought that God has put into that verse for him, and then dwell upon the thought until it becomes his own. One passage thus studied until its significance is clear is of more value than the perusal of many chapters with no definite purpose in view and no positive instruction gained.[4]

Keep in mind that "digging for golden treasure" is not brushing over the surface of the Bible but searching until you find a gem for the day. Sometimes I'll read and find something profound immediately. I'll pray and journal about it and will be blown away at how it speaks to my life. Other times I read a portion of Scripture, and it doesn't hit the mark as much. I've learned to keep reading, to keep digging, because the gems are there to be found. When I dig long enough, I am always sure to find something of great value every single time—even in places like Leviticus.

I came across a quote by Bishop Butler, who says, "Nor is it at all incredible, that a book, which has been so long in the possession of mankind, should contain many truths as yet undiscovered."[5] Digging deeply to find such gems in each verse shows you how profound the Bible is and how it can speak to people of any age.

I've taught my eight-year-old son, Eli, this method and how to keep things simple. These are the steps I have modeled with him, knowing that he will be able to do this himself after some time:

First, find a Bible promise. When I'm working with Eli, I usually find two verses and read them aloud to him. Then I let him choose which one he'd like to explore that day (choice is very important for us all). I invite him to copy the verse, word for word, into his journal, and when he's finished copying it, I ask him to read it aloud. Then I ask him what he thinks the one big idea is, in the verse. (If he's not sure, I ask him to identify the two or three most important words.) He underlines it. I invite him to write down, in his own words, what this big idea is telling him. It could be something about God, him, or the story. If he's stuck, I'll ask him an open question to help his thinking. Finally, I invite him to write down a one-sentence response to God. To conclude, he prays out loud, either with me, or by himself. Then I ask him, "Who can you share this with, today?"

---

4. White, *Education*, 189.

5. Joseph Butler, *Analogy of Religion Natural and Revealed, to the Constitution and Course of Nature* (Cincinnati, OH: Jennings and Graham, 1847), 209.

Kid's Bible Study Guide

1. **Ask Jesus** to be with you as you read.
2. Choose a **Bible verse** or passage.
3. **Write the passage** into your journal. Then read it aloud.
4. **Underline the big idea** in the passage.
5. Write down **what this big idea tells you about God** or **yourself**.
6. Write down (or whisper) a **prayer** of what you want to say to Jesus.

I have included two examples of this. Eli didn't do these especially for this book, but he gave permission for me to use them here. These are real examples from his Bible study journal. He likes to write his name, and in the first example, his birthday and a little picture of himself thinking his prayer to God as well. Isn't he precious? I've also included an example of my own.

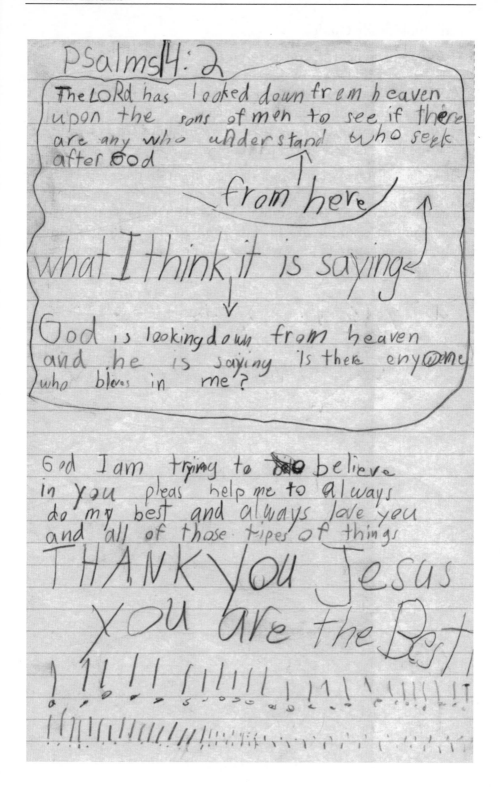

Psalms 14:2

The LORd has looked down frem heaven upon the sons of men to see if there are any who understand who seek after God

from here

what I think it is saying

God is looking down from heaven and he is saying Is there enyone who blievs in me?

God I am trying to believe in you pleas help me to always do my best and always love you and all of those tipes of things

THANK YOU Jesus YOU are the Best

VERSE-BY-VERSE METHOD

Isaiah 51:7-9

"Listen to Me, you who know righteousness,   ] My mind & heart should
You people in whose heart is My law:] listen to God & take courage!
Do not fear the reproach of men,   ] I don't need to worry.
Nor be afraid of their insults.
For the moth will eat them up like a garment,   ] This is why I don't
And the worm will eat them like wool;   ] need to worry.
But My righteousness will be forever,   ] God is
And My salvation from generation to generation.] eternal
Awake, awake, put on strength,   ] I need to wake up and not
O arm of the Lord!   give up. I am part of God's
Awake as in the ancient days,   arm to do His work.
In the generations of old."

Thank You, Lord, for this powerful message.
Thank You for giving me courage today and
this reminder not to worry or be afraid.
Please wake me up so that I can put on Your
strength completely. I'm willing and available
to be Your "arm" today!

For young children who are learning to read, copying a verse from the Bible can be tricky, and they can become frustrated if they skip a word or repeat or miss an entire line. What I've found that works well is to give Eli a little bookmark, which he places horizontally in the Bible directly beneath the line he is copying. It is the bookmark on which I have recorded the five simple steps.

As I've watched my children study their Bibles, I've seen gradual changes occur in their characters. They might be battling in the area of stubbornness or selfishness (as we all do at times), but in the mornings, after they've read, I see a sweet spirit of humility that is only explainable by the change the Bible can bring to our lives. I believe that nothing can transform our hearts and attitudes in such a powerful way as the Holy Spirit who works in us through God's words.

It can be really special for children to read over their Bible study journals whenever they are feeling sad or frustrated, or if they need encouragement. Tahlia, my daughter, is often excited by what she's read because she sees how it connects with her life experience, and through this, she sees that God is real and wants to interact with her. After a recent international move for our family, she was missing her friends and feeling quite sad. But then, day after day she would find me to show me Bible promises that she had found herself that spoke directly to her homesickness and the fact that Jesus had promised He would see her soon. She found these promises and others:

> Trust in the Lord with all your heart
> and lean not on your own understanding;
> in all your ways submit to him,
> and he will make your paths straight. (Proverbs 3:5, 6, NIV)

> "Be strong and of good courage, do not fear nor be afraid of them; for the Lord your God, He is the One who goes with you. He will not leave you nor forsake you." (Deuteronomy 31:6)

> "In My Father's house are many mansions; if it were not so, I would have told you. I go to prepare a place for you." (John 14:2)

> "And behold, I am coming quickly, and My reward is with Me, to give to every one according to his work." (Revelation 22:12)

Revisiting these promises that God had spoken into her life brought her courage and the assurance that God was in control and that He is leading her life. She identified this by herself, which was exciting for her.

As a brief side note, I want to share that the Bible or your child's Bible study journal should never, ever be used as a weapon to coerce their behavior or their minds. If you do this, they may start to resent you and the Bible. Such coercion also goes directly against God's character. The importance of the will is difficult to overstate. The Bible makes it clear that free will is of incredible importance to God. He could have created us with limitations, like a robot, to react to circumstances according to preinstalled programming. Doing this would have gone against the deepest and most important qualities of His character— love and freedom.

If your children cannot write yet, you can still teach them through this method. Share each of the steps, and instead of having them write a response, invite them to respond by drawing a picture or simply talking about the verse with you and God.

2. Word Study

For theologians, a word study usually means using concordances, dictionaries, and other reference books to trace the use of a word through Scripture. However, what I found to be a blessing is to approach a verse simply by considering each word and what it might be saying to me.

To do a word study, I explore a stand-alone verse and consider each of the words, reading the verse multiple times, emphasizing a different word each time. I usually copy out the verse, word by word, multiple times. I then consider the different words in the verse, and write down my thoughts on the meaning of these words. To conclude, I write a prayer response to God about the passage and what it has spoken into my life.

The steps are as follows:

1. Pray for the Holy Spirit to guide your mind and heart as you read.

2. Write out the **same verse multiple times**.

3. Consider the **different words** in the verse.

4. Write **down** your thoughts about **what these words are saying** to you today.

5. Write a **prayer response** to God.

It's an amazing experience to allow God to reveal different messages through one short verse. Here is an example of the first portion of Isaiah 25:9.

WORD STUDY

Isaiah 25:9

Behold, this is our God;
We have waited for Him, and He will save us.
(God is worthy to behold! How can I behold Him more today?)

Behold, this _is_ our God;
We have waited for Him, and He will save us.
(God IS my God - I claim this!)

Behold, this is _our_ God;
We have waited for Him, and He will save us.
(God is not just my God; He is the God of everyone - impartial.)

Behold, this is our Go_d;_
We have waited for Him, and He will save us.
(God is beyond anything else in existence, and He alone is GOD.)

Behold, this is our God;
_We_ have waited for Him, and He will save us.
(For centuries, God's people waited for Him. I now wait a second time.)

Behold, this is our God;
We have _waited_ for Him, and He will save us.
(Waiting is not always easy. Although I wait for His return, I also wait for him to answer some of my prayers. Today I wait, knowing and trusting that He will answer in His time.)

Behold, this is our God;
We have waited for Him, and He _will_ save us.
(There is no doubt in this verse. It's clear what God will do.)

Behold, this is our God;
We have waited for Him, and He will _save_ us.
(Saving me is something only God can do. It's what I most need.)

Behold, this is our God;
We have waited for Him, and He will save _us._
(His salvation is free to everyone, not just me.)

God, You are so very great! This morning I behold You... As the sun rises and the mist hovers above the grass. Today I wait for You to return. I'm also waiting on You to answer me about a few other things as well - You know them. I don't doubt that You will answer, in the same way I know You'll return and save me. I need You in my life today as much as ever. Love you, Lord!

You can see how powerful it is to meditate on a small portion of God's Word. God has spoken truth into my soul on many occasions through this method of simply and prayerfully considering one verse and what that verse speaks into my life that morning. You can see how simple it is to consider the meaning, word by word, and to respond to the verse upon conclusion.

3. Book or Chapter Study

Another of my favorite ways of studying the Bible is to choose a book of the Bible and study it passage by passage or chapter by chapter. It's really an expansion of the verse-by-verse method. This kind of study takes a little more time, especially if you want to meditate on the Word and study it rather than do a rushed reading, but, as with the verse-by-verse method, it is deeply rewarding and relationship building.

For this approach, I follow these steps:

1. **Pray:** Before you begin, pray for the Holy Spirit to guide your mind and your heart as you read.

2. **Read:** As you slowly read the chapter, underline any big ideas that stand out to you.

3. **Reflect and rewrite:** Reflect on the verses and ideas you've underlined, and rewrite these in your journal.

4. **Relate:** What is God saying directly to you through this passage? Reflect and respond in your journal.

5. **Pray:** Write a personal prayer response to God.

It's often helpful to use a Bible dictionary or commentary if you want to dig deeper into the chapter. However, I always read the plain text and respond in worship first.

BOOK/CHAPTER STUDY

Numbers 9: 15 - 23

vs. 17. "Whenever the cloud was taken up from above the
tabernacle, after that the children of Israel would
journey; and in the place where the cloud settled,
there the children of Israel would pitch their tents."

vs. 18 "At the command of the Lord the children of Israel
would journey, and at the command of the Lord
they would camp; as long as the cloud stayed
above the tabernacle they remained encamped."

What an incredible chapter this is! I love what this tells me
about trusting God and His ways. The children of Israel
only moved when the cloud moved. This means they would
have had to be prepared to move every single day.
They didn't really settle into one area too comfortably
because God had a plan for them. Although it took much
longer than they (or God!) wanted, their goal was to move
until they reached their new "home."
        The people didn't know where the cloud would
move to next. I wonder if they ever stood at the edge of
the shadow from the cloud, wanting and wishing it would move?
Or if they groaned when it stopped and moved, stopped and
moved, many days in a row?
        Lord, I am like the children of Israel. I want to watch
for the cloud - for You - to direct every movement of my life.
But while I wait beneath your cloud, help me not to grumble!
I know the place where I am is the place where You want
me to be. Give me greater faith to trust You in this, Lord.
Help me not to run in front of Your cloud of leading in
my life. I know that whether I'm in a desolate wilderness
or by a spring of cool water, You're teaching me and preparing
me for home.

4. Big Questions

I believe that any biblical passage can speak into our lives when we come in open humility and prayer. Sometimes you may want to consider asking some big questions to deepen your understanding of the passage. Take, for example, these three questions, which I find always bring personal insight and challenge:

1. What does this passage tell me about God?

2. What does this passage tell me about myself and humanity?

3. What change will I make today as a result of understanding God's word?

There are other big questions that you can apply to a passage to deepen your understanding of it. These questions can be asked to help you dig deeper into any story or chapter:

4. What does this passage or story tell me about the great controversy between good and evil?

5. Where can I see the work of redemption (God saving humankind) in this passage or story?

6. What other passages can I find that further expand on these themes?

I appreciate the following quote in light of these questions:

> The Bible is its own expositor. Scripture is to be compared with scripture. The student should learn to view the word as a whole, and to see the relation of its parts. He should gain a knowledge of its grand central theme, of God's original purpose for the world, of the rise of the great controversy, and of the work of redemption. He should understand the nature of the two principles that are contending for supremacy, and should learn to trace their working through the records of history and prophecy, to the great consummation. He should see how this controversy enters into every phase of human experience; how in every act of life he himself reveals the one or the other of the two antagonistic motives; and how, whether he will or not, he is even now deciding upon which side of the controversy he will be found.[6]

Seeing the Bible through different lenses shows how deep you can dig to find that golden treasure we talked about.

---

6. White, *Education*, 190.

BIG QUESTIONS.

Luke 10:38-42. (Mary & Martha.)

1. What does this passage tell me about God?
   Jesus, God in human form, interracted with humanity in a
   very personal way. He ate, taught, walked and socialized
   with men and women — with the goal to show them
   the truth about His father, and the reason He'd come to earth.
   I love that Jesus uses Martha's name here twice. He acknowledges
   how she is feeling and speaks to her about a different,
   better way.

2. What does this passage tell me about myself/humanity?
   This story speaks so powerfully into our 21st Century lives.
   We are too busy — I am too busy! Often I'm consumed
   by the many "good" busy things at the expense of time
   with Jesus — the most important Person.

3. What change will I make today as a result of
   understanding God's Word?
      Jesus' words "Mary has chosen that good part, which
   will not be taken away from her" (vs. 42) really
   stands out to me. It tells me that I can allow myself
   to be swallowed up in my business, or I can choose
   to spend time with Jesus.
         So often I am worried and troubled by many
   things — just like Martha — when really these things
   are probably not worth worrying about.
         Today, I choose to sit first at Jesus' feet.
   I choose Him before everything else.

BIG QUESTIONS CONT...

Luke 10:38-42   (Mary & Martha)

4. What does this story tell me about the great controversy between good and evil?
   There is a battle over my time and thoughts — although I rarely think about this. Jesus invites me to choose to sit at His feet, but too often I give in to other distractions.

5. Where can I see the work of redemption in this story?
   There is an open invitation for humankind to sit at Jesus' feet. While some people are already at His feet, Jesus invites all to come and join Him. He doesn't give up on us, even when we are distracted, overworked or too busy. He wants everyone to sit down with Him.

6. What other passages can I find that further expand on this theme?
   The first passage that came to my mind was Matt 6:25-34, about "Do not worry."
   I love vs 33-34 in particular.
   I also think of John 3:16, 17. God sent Jesus so that whoever — that means anyone — believes might be saved. He didn't come to condemn, but to save.

> Jesus, I sit at your feet now, and although I have to start my day, I actually want to remain at your feet throughout the day. Show me ways I can seek you in all that I do today.

5. Who, Where, When, What, Why?

These five simple questions are particularly useful when you want to explore the context and the meaning of what the story can teach you for today. Using a commentary, study Bible, or Bible concordance can be very helpful. For personal enrichment, I particularly like to use the Conflict of the Ages series (*Patriarchs and Prophets, Prophets and Kings, The Desire of Ages,* and *The Acts of the Apostles*) by Ellen White when using this method to study. Her commentary on the biblical narratives is deeply rich, insightful, and heart-stirring.

WHO? WHERE? WHEN? WHAT? WHY?

Numbers 20:14-21

1. Who are the key people in this story?
   Moses, his messengers, the king of Edom, Israel.

2. Where did this story take place?
   The children of Israel were camped only a short distance
   away from the border of Edom, near Canaan, the Promised Land.

3. When did this happen in relation to other big events in the Bible?
   Moses led the Israelites out of Egypt to journey to a new home –
   Canaan. This happened closer to the end of their long journey.
   The people were tired of walking through the desert. They
   longed to be "home."

4. What happened in this story?
   Moses wanted to travel through the land of Edom to get
   to Canaan. He sent messengers to politely ask the king if
   they could pass through. They said they wouldn't take or
   destroy anything – they wouldn't even drink their water!
   The king's response was a strong "NO."
   Israel's messengers asked a second time, and again were
   told "No," and that they would be met with the sword.
   And so, Israel had to go back into the desert, to journey
   around Edom.
   　　Patriarchs & Prophets says this (pp. 422, 423)
   "Had the people, when brought into trial, trusted in God,
   the Captain of the Lord's host would have led them
   through Edom...
   　　It is important to believe God's word and act upon it
   promptly, while His angels are waiting to work for us. Evil angels are
   ready to contest every step of advance... God's servants should be
   minutemen, ever ready to move as fast as His providence opens the way.
   Any delay on their part gives time for Satan to work to defeat them."
   (Emphasis added.)

As you study a passage, consider the following questions:

- **Who** are the key people in this story or passage? (What do they tell me?)
- **Where** did this story take place? (How might knowing the location add to the story?)
- **When** did this happen in relation to other big events in the Bible? (What is the context of the story?)
- **What** happened in this story? (What is the big message of this story?)
- **Why** might this story or passage have been included in the Bible? (What does it say to me today?)

Using this approach will help you to see a story with new eyes.

---

5. Why might this story have been included in the Bible?
(What does it speak to me, today?)

From Patriarchs & Prophets pp. 421-423

The Edomites were descendants of Abraham and Isaac. God had given them Mt. Seir, and while Israel was to destroy the inhabitants of Canaan, they were to spare the Edomites.
God had actually intended for them to pass through Edom, to be a blessing to the Edomites by showing them what it's like to follow God.

God's people should have — trusted God
— acted promptly.

Satan had been distracting them, pointing out the many challenges along the way and had stripped them of their full confidence in God's leading them home.

If only they had remembered God's leading throughout their journey! It makes me think back to the beginning ... "The Lord will fight for you, and you shall hold your peace." (Ex 14.14)

Lead me through Edom today, Lord. Past any enemies. Help me to act promptly, and please provide the Captain, to lead me through Edom.

6. Claiming Promises as My Personal Prayers

The words in the Bible can encourage you like nothing else in the world can. I've had times in my life when I've been searching and God has directly and clearly spoken to me and given me answers through what I've read in the Bible. Other times I've been lonely or discouraged and have found the greatest comfort from the Bible.

There are certain passages or chapters that I read regularly when I need certain encouragement from God. You may also have a list of go-to chapters, but I thought I'd share mine with you. This list is by no means an exhaustive but, rather, some examples of where to start. They are ours to claim!

- God's love for me, a sinner: Hosea 11; John 3:16, 17; Jude 24, 25
- Assurance that God is leading: Daniel 2:20–23; Ecclesiastes 3:1–15; Psalm 31
- Feeling lonely or sad: Matthew 5:3–12; Philippians 4:4–8; 4:19
- Guidance on how to live: Jeremiah 31:33; Exodus 20; Micah 6:8; 1 Corinthians 13; Colossians 3:12–17
- Praising God: Psalm 67; Job 37
- Feeling stressed or worried: Luke 12:22–34; Hebrews 13:5, 6; 1 Peter 5:6, 7
- Living like a Christian: Romans 12:9–21; Ephesians 5:8–14; 1 John 1:7; 2:15–17
- Seeking wisdom from God: Proverbs 2:1–9
- Feeling scared: Psalm 91; 57:1–3
- Fighting the enemy: Ephesians 6:10–20; 1 Peter 5:8–11
- Wanting to repent: Psalm 51; 2 Timothy 2:19–22
- Realizing I am in need of a Savior: John 6:41–51; Ephesians 2:4–10
- Seeking Jesus more: Jeremiah 24:7; 29:11–14
- God is more powerful than my circumstances: Isaiah 55; Zephaniah 3:16, 17
- Needing to fix my eyes on eternity rather than what is before me: Isaiah 65:17–25; 1 Thessalonians 4:15–18; Revelation 21; 22
- Needing boldness to speak for God: Isaiah 55:11; 59:21; 2 Timothy 1:8–12; 4:2–5; 1 Peter 3:13–17
- For healing (spiritual or physical): Isaiah 58:8; 2 Corinthians 4:16–18; James 5:13–16

CLAIMING PROMISES AS MY
PERSONAL PRAYERS.

vs. 1-3   In You, O Lord, I put my trust;
Let me never be ashamed;
Deliver me in Your righteousness.
Bow down Your ear to me,   I know You hear me, Lord.
Deliver me speedily;
Be my rock of refuge,   I trust You, God. I trust You to
A fortress of defense to save me.   lead our future, though it seems
For You are my rock and my fortress;   uncertain. You are my
Therefore, for Your name's sake,   certainty—My Rock, my Refuge.
Lead me and guide me...

vs. 14,15 But as for me, I trust in You, O Lord;
I say, "You are my God."
My times are in Your hand.   I commit my times, my future,

v. 16.   Make Your face shine upon Your   to You. Shine on me. Give me
servant...   assurance and peace that You will

19-20   Oh, how great is Your goodness,   lead, as You have in the past.
Which You have laid up for those who   I've known and seen Your
fear You,   great goodness, time and time
Which You have prepared for those   again. You prepare what is best,
who trust in You   only the best! — for me. I trust
In the presence of the sons of men!   You, and Your plans.
You shall hide them in the secret place
of Your presence...

v. 24   Be of good courage,   Give me courage today, Lord.
And He shall strengthen your heart,   Make my heart strong
All you who hope in the Lord.   in the knowledge and peace
that You are leading me.

Thank You, my God, Best Friend,
and the One who alone leads me
and saves me.

It's one thing to read these beautiful promises and to claim them as our own. But I find that when I copy a short passage or chapter word for word into my journal, I meditate on it in a deeper way than if I just read it. And so, when life's circumstances particularly challenge me, I often write out a passage word by word in my journal, and then I write a response (which is really my heart's prayer) alongside the verses that are particularly meaningful to me. You can see an example below from Psalm 31. In this example, I have focused particularly on the verses that spoke to me (you will see the verses listed beside the text on the left-hand side.)

Keep Things Vibrant

I've read the same passages over and over, and they always seem to hold new meaning, depending on my season of life. The Bible is such a rich, deep book that I can't imagine ever getting tired of studying it. But if it seems as though your daily time with God is getting repetitive, try some of the following:

- Go for a walk in nature and listen to a portion of the Bible on audio. Take a pen and a small notepad with you and pause to write down any big ideas as you listen.

- Print out an entire book (e.g., John) and mark it with different colors and symbols. For example, you might add a question mark for something you don't understand; an asterisk beside something you really like; and a plus sign beside something that points to Jesus. Explore each verse slowly, using a Bible commentary or Bible dictionary.

- Read the Bible aloud, and imagine God reading it to you.

- Hide yourself away somewhere for a few hours and read an entire book of the Bible in one sitting. Start with some of the smaller New Testament books, but challenge yourself to read some of the larger books too. I've read both Matthew and Revelation in one sitting, and it was a truly profound experience.

- Compare a paraphrase with your usual Bible translation. Write down new insights you find.

- Meet with a friend and read the Bible together, aloud. Journal individually, and then share insights with each other. Sharing this with someone may raise new questions or ideas that you can explore together.

- Choose a Bible story you know well but consider the perspective of a lesser character. Reread the story in a few different versions, and consider the viewpoint of that character. What can be learned from them and applied to your life today?

- Consider studying with someone who can read the original languages, along with a concordance and Bible dictionary, to dig deeply into the message of a passage.

In the same way that we keep our friendships alive with variety and new adventures, keep your daily appointment with God fresh and vibrant by using different methods to help you to see new perspectives.

Sweeter Than Honey

A few months ago a friend gave me a slab of honeycomb from their beehive. I'd never tried honeycomb before and wasn't even exactly sure how to eat it. I took a teaspoon, sank it into the soft honeycomb holes and scooped a generous heap into my mouth. I was surprised at how the sweet honey melted on my tongue, and as I gently chewed on the wax before spitting it out, I marveled at how delicious it was! I ate the rest of that honeycomb in less than a week! It was so scrumptious that I would have to say that other than maple syrup, honeycomb is my new favorite dessert.

Having recently eaten honeycomb, I found that Psalm 119:103, 104 had new meaning for me:

> How sweet are Your words to my taste,
> Sweeter than honey to my mouth!
> Through Your precepts I get understanding.

God's words are indeed sweet to my soul and unlike anything else the world offers me.

These few examples that I shared are among the ones that I use as I've gone from reading to studying my Bible. They show what I do most days to spend time with God in His Word. I find these simple approaches allow me to reflect on His Word, and they provide an opportunity for it to speak into my life in a very personal way.

Studying my Bible like this has deepened my knowledge of God and His work in the world and my life, but what's most important is that it has greatly deepened my relationship with Him as never before. I know I can go to the Bible for guidance for my life, and I can also turn to God's Word to praise Him. Worshiping Him, learning about Him, and leaning on Him through His Word is wonderfully life changing.

Share!

Whatever you do to keep your personal Bible study fresh, one thing will keep it alive for you: sharing the gems you've discovered.

Every day after I spend time in God's Word, when the Holy Spirit either convicts me of something in my life or shows me something I've never seen or thought of before, I want to share it with someone. The first person I want to tell is Matt, my amazing husband. It's exciting because there's always something new, even from the old stories that I grew up with. He also shares his insights with me. It's inspiring to see God speaking into someone else's life through His Word, and I love hearing what Matt shares.

The Bible is the richest, most profound book to me because there is always more to discover. When I share my discoveries, not only do they solidify in my mind, but I hear Matt's thoughts, and we wrestle through our findings together. He asks questions or shares thoughts I'd not considered and also shares what he's studied. It's a rich conversation that revitalizes both mind and heart.

Nothing has deepened my marriage more than this. It amazes me how sharing biblical truths deepens relationships as nothing else in the world can. Matt and I share in spontaneous ways—over breakfast, while I'm making lunch, and often in front of our children. We've always wanted our children to see that our walk with God is living and vibrant and daily—and while our sharing is not contrived, we happily share before our family.

If you are dating someone, I encourage you to share the gems you're discovering in the Bible with your boyfriend or girlfriend. While you don't want to make any spiritual judgments, you will very quickly see how spiritually compatible you are and whether the other person is open to hearing and growing with you. Whom you choose to marry is perhaps the biggest contributing factor to your future walk with God, and your future into eternity. Sharing with each other in this way will allow God to lead in this important decision.

I can't help looking for ways to share the wonderful insights I've found in my Bible each morning—to encourage someone or invite them to turn to God for advice and support. I'm often amazed at how my personal Bible study directly affects conversations each day. I do not doubt that when I start my day by abiding in Christ, my actions, my thoughts, and my conversations are always different as a result of the time I've spent with Him.

How Long Should I Study?

Studying your Bible can take minutes or hours, depending on how much you grapple with God's Word. As with any relationship, the longer you spend with someone, the more you get to know them. It's the same with God. You might find it hard to spend fifteen minutes initially, but over time you might be surprised at how time slips away when you're spending time lingering with a great Friend.

You'll be encouraged as you spend time with God, no matter whether you find yourself in a spiritual valley or on a mountaintop. So make time, no matter how busy you are. This appointment is one you can't afford to miss! It's not necessarily important to keep a stopwatch to make sure you spend a certain amount of time studying your Bible; it's more important that you try to meet with God daily, just as you would with a friend you're getting to know. It might seem hard, like a one-sided relationship, since you can't see or touch God, but His Word is living, and when you ask Him, His Holy Spirit will be right there with you as you read.

You will have times when you feel as though you're not getting much from your daily devotions, and you may want to give up. But hear me on this, and I've said it before—if you studied your Bible only when you felt like it, you would rarely study it! The devil would make sure you never felt like it. Our feelings come and go, but the Word of God endures forever, and most important, your relationship with Him will endure forever (1 Peter 1:25).

If you find yourself struggling to spend time with God, consider whether any of the following factors are affecting your time in God's Word:

- **Lack of sleep**. Are you getting enough rest?

- **Business**. Are you too busy? What can you eliminate or reduce so that you can concentrate on the important things?

- **Stuck**. Are you feeling stale in your devotion time? How can you mix things up to keep it relevant?

- **Hidden sins**. Are you involved in something you need to confess that is keeping you away from God?

- **Share**. Are you sharing what you're learning? If not, start to! It will give you a greater sense of purpose in your study.

If you miss a day, don't get discouraged. Don't let that stop you from coming to meet with God the next day. He will be waiting for you. Of course, don't make too many exceptions, because we all know how easy it is to justify our lack of commitment to Bible study with other "good" things in our lives. Since being with God is our daily spiritual bread, our souls need it every day. It's a staple for our lives.

Finally, one thing I wish I could say to you in person: *It's impossible to overstate how much spending time with God in His word will change your life.* God wants this more than anything else. He wants you to know Him for who He really is. He wants to give peace to your weary heart, strength to your mind, and courage to your soul. David, a man after God's own heart, testifies of this: "Taste and see that the LORD is good. Oh, the joys of those who take refuge in him!" (Psalm 34:8, NLT).

At the end of the day, your relationship with God is between you and God. Will you commit to studying your Bible for twenty-one days? They say it takes twenty-one days to break a bad habit and about the same amount of time to form a new one. Ask God to help you to keep this appointment (if possible, in the morning) and see Him work in and through your life in amazing ways.

7

Digging in Together

And let us consider how to stir up one another to love and good works,
not neglecting to meet together, as is the habit of some, but encouraging one another,
and all the more as you see the Day drawing near.
Hebrews 10:24-25, ESV

A couple of years ago, my husband, Matt, was at a church meeting, and I was home having dinner with our three cherubs. The day had been unusually busy, and the kids were more active than they had been in a long time. As we sat down at the table to eat, they started to bicker, to push and fight and say unkind words. I sat down and watched them, feeling frustrated because they seemed unusually harsh. I looked out the window and could almost see the smirk of the devil as he laughed at my frustration with my children—the very children God has loaned to me to love and to teach to follow Him.

As they continued to squabble, I sat in silence, praying for patience and wisdom and that the Holy Spirit would come and be among us. Then a thought occurred to me. What would happen if I spoke God's Word into the lives of my children at this moment? In my heart I wanted God to be present among us. What if I invited Him there on behalf of my children?

I said a Bible verse out loud and asked the kids whether they'd heard it before. I wrote it on a piece of paper for each of them so that they could hold a copy of the verse. Then I asked them each a question about the verse, and we talked about it for a few minutes while we were eating. The question I asked my five-year-old was simple, and then I asked my other two older children a slightly more complex question. Then I shared some thoughts about the verse.

I was amazed at the transformation in the tone in our home. It went from chaos to peace, and it was as though God Himself had come to sit at our table to be with us. It reminded me of this quote: "A change wrought by the word, it is one of the deepest mysteries of the word. We cannot understand it; we can only believe, as declared by the Scriptures, it is 'Christ in you, the hope of glory.' Colossians 1:27."[1]

This experience reminded me that the direct piece of advice given to families in Deuteronomy 6:4–9 is practical advice:

> "Hear, O Israel: The LORD our God, the LORD is one! You shall love the LORD your God with all your heart, with all your soul, and with all your strength.
>
> "And these words which I command you today shall be in your heart. You shall teach them diligently to your children, and shall talk of them when you sit in your house, when you walk by the way, when you lie down, and when you rise up. You shall bind them as a sign on your hand, and they shall be as frontlets between your eyes. You shall write them on the doorposts of your house and on your gates."

God wants us to bring His words into every aspect of our daily lives. He wants more than a one-off worship thought in the mornings or evenings, although this is very important also. He doesn't want to be compartmentalized into moments or days in time. He wants to be part of our daily living—our conversations, our challenges, our big events, and our everyday moments.

Some Jews take this command very seriously and literally by sticking the law on their doorposts, their foreheads, and their wrists. But what is God's message for us here? Perhaps the reality of our answer is this: "In order to interest our children in the Bible, we ourselves must be interested in it. To awaken in them a love for its study, we must love it. Our instruction to them will have only the weight of influence given it by our own example and spirit."[2]

---

1. White, *Education*, 172.

2. White, *Education*, 187.

We've spent some time exploring how to engage in personal Bible study individually and with our children, but take a moment to consider these questions:

- How interested am I in the Bible for myself?

- Do I enjoy reading it or studying it? Do I *love* it, as the verse suggests?

- How does reading my Bible change my day, my attitudes, my conversations, and my thoughts?

- Can reading the Bible together at home change the conversations in my home and the way I speak to my family? Am I willing to try it?

When God's words are in our hearts, it *does* change our actions and what our minds think about. It can dramatically change our relationships and the atmosphere of our homes.

Maybe you find it hard to talk with your family about spiritual things. It's interesting that our family members can be (or should be) some of the closest people in our lives, yet they can often be the most difficult people to talk to about God. They see us in our lowest, rawest moments; when we take off our masks and stop seeking to impress or pretend. They see us warts and all. And sometimes it seems difficult to find time to purposefully bring talk about God into your home. I'm encouraged that I'm not the only one who feels this way. "It requires much patience and spirituality to bring Bible religion into the home life . . . , to bear the strain of worldly business, and yet keep the eye single to the glory of God."[3]

How can we follow the advice in Deuteronomy? Where do we start? I believe it comes down to open conversation about what the Bible speaks into our lives.

Jesus loved having deep, profound conversations with those around Him. Some of these conversations were short and thought-provoking (Matthew 8:18–22; 9:10–13), while other conversations were longer. We can have short, thought-provoking conversations about the Bible with our families, too.

Having conversations around the messages in the Bible doesn't always feel natural, and the last thing you want is for such discussions to feel contrived. Instead, you want them to be the natural overflow of personal time with Him. Carefully and prayerfully consider the character of your

---

3. White, *The Desire of Ages*, 73.

child and the mood of the moment when bringing the Bible into your conversations. (And of course, we must never use Scripture or spiritual conversations to punish or manipulate in any way, as this goes against God's very nature, as I mentioned before.)

After my experience at the dinner table with my children, something I have done in more recent times is to give a physical copy of a Bible verse (the same verse) to each family member to reflect on. The subsequent conversation can be done at the dinner table, in the car, before bed, or even when we're going for a walk. The conversations that arise are not part of our daily family worship times but are more spontaneous conversations about the Bible.

I call these physical copies of Bible verses POP (purpose of passage) cards because, as in a popcorn prayer, each person shares a short thought about the purpose of the passage and how God is speaking into their lives through it. There's something about holding a nice card in your hand that allows you to read and reread the verse that can bring greater clarity or depth of thought in comparison to listening to someone else recite or read a verse. ("See Appendix for some examples of POP cards.")

I invite my family to silently read the verse I've given them, and then I ask someone to read it out loud. Then, starting with the youngest family member, I ask a simple question about the verse. After they have responded, I invite each person to share something about the verse that they may have noticed, and finally, I share something about the verse too.

For example, the card you give each person might have 2 Samuel 22:29, 31 on it:

> "For You are my lamp, O LORD;
> The LORD shall enlighten my darkness. . . .
> As for God, His way is perfect;
> The word of the Lord is proven;
> He is a shield to all who trust in Him."

As each person holds a copy of the verse, you might ask questions such as:

- Have you ever been afraid of the dark?

- What makes the dark scary?

- How could God be our lamp?

- When have you doubted that God's way is perfect?

• When have you trusted in God's way?

• What do you need God to shield you from today?

Then I (or someone else) will share a brief takeaway thought, and we pray together about what we have discussed. Each person can keep the POP card, or I collect it to use again in the future.

We may spend only a few moments talking about the verse, or we may spend twenty minutes, but talking about the Bible as a family is a deeper level of conversation than usual. It binds us together! I think it also shows my kids that the Bible is rich and worth digging into. This quote shares this idea well:

> It is impossible for any human mind to exhaust even one truth or promise of the Bible. One catches the glory from one point of view, another from another point; yet we can discern only gleamings.[4]

What I love is that spending time as a family, talking about God's messages in just one Bible verse, also opens up intergenerational faith talk, something that doesn't always happen naturally in a church setting without a lot of planning and thought.

wTalking about the Bible doesn't have to be limited to a family with children. If you're single or dating, you could use a Bible verse POP card as an icebreaker with friends over dinner. If you're married, you could use these POP cards over breakfast before beginning a busy day. You can use these cards with anyone, anywhere if you want to encourage biblical faith talk. The purpose of this experience is to talk about the Bible and how it applies to your life *today*, on a deeper level than usual, with people you care about.

Ultimately, these POP cards show us how the purpose of God's Word is to speak into our twenty-first-century lives in real ways. God is not distant and removed but is ever-present and wants to be involved in our day-to-day lives and conversations. Will you intentionally invite Him to do so?

Family Worship

You may have noticed before in your life that when we talk about godly things, something special happens to our relationships. It might

---

4. White, *Education*, 171.

take some days or even weeks, but pray and look for the change that God's Word will bring to your life and your family. Modeling an honest, open walk with God is one of the best gifts you could give your family. It doesn't matter whether you know a lot about the Bible or not much at all. No matter how little you've read the Bible or how often you've read it, there is still so much more that can be learned about God by reading it.

Here's some advice about family worship:

> The hours of morning and evening worship should be the sweetest and most helpful of the day. Let it be understood that into these hours no troubled, unkind thoughts are to intrude; that parents and children assemble to meet with Jesus, and to invite into the home the presence of holy angels. Let the services be brief and full of life, adapted to the occasion, and varied from time to time. Let all join in the Bible reading and learn and often repeat God's law. It will add to the interest of the children if they are sometimes permitted to select the reading. Question them upon it, and let them ask questions. Mention anything that will serve to illustrate its meaning.[5]

So, here is the advice we're given for family worship in a nutshell:

• Make it a daily occurrence that includes prayer.

• Keep this time free of stress and frustration (angels are among us during this time).

• Keep it short, and it shouldn't be too predictable.

• Feature the Bible each time. Everyone can repeat the verse. (Sometimes kids should be allowed to choose what to read.)

• Include questions (to be asked and answered) about the Bible verses. These questions will bring meaning into everyday life.

What barriers are preventing you from having daily worship? For us, setting a specific time in the morning and evening when we would meet as a family was an essential step.

How can you set aside a time for worship with minimal stress and rush? I've found that playing some quiet, relaxing music in the background helps a lot with this.

---

5. White, *Education*, 186.

What can you do for family worship? Sometimes not having an idea or a plan can be the biggest barrier. You might have tried devotional books but found they don't quite hit the mark for all family members, or you might have read a story that you discover is not age appropriate, so you've had to abandon it. We've read The Bible Story books to our young children multiple times. This ten-part series has brought insight to all of us, and it's biblical. We also love reading inspiring mission stories. Variety is the key!

How can you include each family member in your worship time while exploring something from the Bible? The POP cards is one example, and they will hopefully give you some ideas as to how you can continue this habit with your family.

Finally, if you haven't been making family worship a daily priority, why don't you start today? It may feel unnatural at first, and you may encounter some resistance from some in your family. But after a while, when it becomes a natural part of your day, I don't doubt that it will become a binding agent for all of you. God is waiting, longing for your family to bask in Him. The blessings will linger into eternity.

8

Sap, Growth, and Dead Branches

I have come that they may have life,
and that they may have it more abundantly.
John 10:10

When my family lived in Michigan, we loved the four defined seasons—the balmy summers, the incredible colors of the fall, the white winters, and the beautiful spring. We embraced every season, and nothing, not even the icy winters, could keep us inside for long. I must say, though, that we heartily welcomed spring every year. We eagerly waited and watched for the new shoots in our garden—for the lily of the valley, the daffodils and tulips and lilacs. No matter how many times I saw the growth of spring after the death of winter, we still marveled at how God brings life every year.

One spring, our kids raced in through the front door, excitedly telling us about some sweet juice that was dripping from a tree. We followed them outside to a maple tree and realized it was maple sap that was dripping from the wood. Matt found some maple syrup equipment in the house we'd bought and set it up. It didn't take long for a small bucket to be filled, and we started the process of boiling it down to make the delicious syrup. It was an exciting task! The small cup of sweet syrup we held at the end was like liquid gold to us! The few weeks' window of opportunity to tap maple sap reminded me of how incredible God is to allow sap to run up through dry, seemingly dead tree trunks and branches to bring forth new shoots and leaves.

It also reminded me of something Jesus said right before He was taken to be crucified. He had left the upper room and walked down the Kidron Valley toward Gethsemane. There Jesus paused, perhaps by a vine, and shared a powerful message with His disciples—the secret of a vibrant relationship with Him. His message was about sap, growth, and dead branches.

"I am the true vine, and my Father is the vinedresser. Every branch in me that does not bear fruit he takes away, and every branch that does bear fruit he prunes, that it may bear more fruit. Already you are clean because of the word that I have spoken to you. Abide in me, and I in you. As the branch cannot bear fruit by itself, unless it abides in the vine, neither can you, unless you abide in me. I am the vine; you are the branches. Whoever abides in me and I in him, he it is that bears much fruit, for apart from me you can do nothing. If anyone does not abide in me he is thrown away like a branch and withers; and the branches are gathered, thrown into the fire, and burned. If you abide in me, and my words abide in you, ask whatever you wish, and it will be done for you. By this my Father is glorified, that you bear much fruit and so prove to be my disciples. As the Father has loved me, so have I loved you. Abide in my love. If you keep my commandments, you will abide in my love, just as I have kept my Father's commandments and abide in his love. These things I have spoken to you, that my joy may be in you, and that your joy may be full.

"This is my commandment, that you love one another as I have loved you. Greater love has no one than this, that someone lay down his life for his friends. You are my friends if you do what I command you. No longer do I call you servants for the servant does not know what his master is doing; but I have called you friends, for all that I have heard from my Father I have made known to you. You did not choose me, but I chose you and appointed you that you should go and bear fruit and that your fruit should abide, so that whatever you ask the Father in my name, he may give it to you" (John 15:1–16, ESV).

Jesus still speaks these words into your heart and mine today. Imagine Jesus looking straight into your eyes, speaking these words to you. What most stands out to you in His words? Perhaps you might want to under-line the big ideas in the passage.

One word is repeated eleven times in this passage. Eleven times! Clearly, Jesus wanted to emphasize this word. It is the word *abide*. Look again at that word in the passage above. What is Jesus saying? He extends an invitation to you and to me to abide in Him. He shares this because He knows that we need to abide in Him more than anything else in this life.

The word *abide* means to accept or act in accordance with.[1] When I think about my marriage, I think of moments when I am closely connected with Matt in every way, and then other times, very rarely, when I've felt a little distant from him. Any distance between us is usually a result of one of us not wanting to accept something the other person has said, or not wanting to do what the other person wants to do. The natural result is tension and discord. You've felt this, too, in your relationships. The good news is that you can abide again, even after feeling distant. All it takes is for one person to seek to bridge the gap between you, and abiding is possible again.

In our relationship with Jesus, He is always seeking to bridge the gap.

When I think of abiding in the context of that relationship, these questions come to mind:

Accept: Do I accept Jesus Christ in my life? Am I surrendered?

Act: Am I acting in accordance with God's desire for my life? Am I spending time with Him in His Word, not just reading but deeply studying it for myself?

Abiding in Christ (through prayer and Bible study) can sometimes seem like one of the hardest things to do. We might know in our minds that it's what we need; we might want to abide. But the rush of life pulls us into its stream, and it all feels too hard. Following God can seem like the biggest burden ever for people who feel obliged or forced by someone else to follow Him. This kind of religion is like slavery because it's all about the external actions rather than what's in the heart. Nothing could be further from what God desires—a relationship whose foundation is mutual love, not just rules; a chosen relationship (in which He first chose you!) based on love and free choice.

At other times, we might be connected to the Vine but not abide in Him. We might be externally connected to the Vine through what we do (our church-going, prayers, conversations, and actions), but inside we

---

1. *English: Oxford Living Dictionaries*, s.v. "abide," accessed August 10, 2018, https://en.oxforddictionaries.com/definition/abide.

feel dead. If we are resisting the Holy Spirit in some way, the sap will stop flowing, and while it might *look* like we're abiding, the evidence will be in our lack of fruit, and eventually, our branches will completely dry up.

Sometimes we might have no desire to abide, but we go through the motions anyway. In times like these, we need to ask God to give us a desire for Him, a longing for our emptiness to be filled, and a nudge to open up and then linger in His Word. When we truly spend time with God with a humble and open heart, through prayer and in His Word, we will be revived.

Let me tell you; I can't *make* myself abide in Jesus any more than a branch can make itself connect to a vine. Abiding happens when we choose to welcome the Holy Spirit into our lives from a conscious choice and an open heart. The amazing thing is that He chose us before we chose Him! He loved us first; He made the first move. Before you or I were born, He loved us; He had a plan to know us and for us to know Him. He seeks us out, like a good Shepherd. My response is always a reaction to what God has done for me.

In addition to this, the great news is that God's actions toward us both precede our decision and follow it. This means that if we choose to prayerfully and humbly spend time with God in His Word, we will not walk away emptyhanded because He will act! He will speak! His word will not return to Him void!

The choice we make each day of how to live our lives, of how we spend our time and whom we give our allegiance to, shows that we are truly free human beings. Will you choose God every morning, even before you swing your legs over the side of your bed to get up? Will you say in your heart, "Today I choose You, Lord. I choose to abide in You; to spend time with you in Your inspired Word." Will you choose Him? The fact is, He chose us first. What an incredible God!

The Sap

It's fascinating to look at how a grapevine survives through winter. In very simple terms, the buds on the branches are dehydrated and isolated from the growing system until spring. When the soil warms up, the roots absorb water, and sap flows up through the trunk of the vine to the buds to initiate growth. Without the sap flowing through the vine, no growth would happen.

The sap in a grapevine is like the Holy Spirit in our lives. We might be like a dead branch, but when we choose to spend time with God, the Holy Spirit pours into us like the sap from the roots (God's Word) and brings us life, and we start to grow.

In the same way that we need to choose to abide in Jesus, we also must ask for the Holy Spirit (the sap) to flow into our lives. Jesus tells us, "If you then, being evil, know how to give good gifts to your children, how much more will your heavenly Father give the Holy Spirit to those who ask Him!" (Luke 11:13). It's the Holy Spirit (this sap) that guides us into all truth (John 16:13) as we spend time with God in His Word. It's this Holy Spirit (the sap) that brings growth and ensures we are connected.

Growth and Fruit

A branch cannot be somewhat connected to a vine. Once you're connected, growth will be the natural result. It's comforting to know that it takes time for a wilted or nearly dead branch to grow leaves, and finally fruit, in the same way that growing in Jesus also takes time. It will happen if you let it.

When our family bought a house in Michigan, we noticed that a vine was growing in our yard. It was wintertime, and no leaves were on the seemingly dead branches. Spring came, and shoots started to grow. We excitedly identified the vine as a grapevine and wondered what sort of grapes might appear, having never grown a grapevine before. Then, over the summer, small, dark purple grapes grew. When we finally tasted the grapes, we identified them as Concord grapes. They were so-o-o-o-o sweet, some of the sweetest grapes we've ever tasted. The growing leaves and then the fruit had confirmed what type of vine it was. It also confirmed that the branches, which we thought were dead, were actually abiding in the vine.

When I stood by our vine that was laden with purple grapes, I felt kind of proud in a small way that we had such a grapevine growing in our yard. It certainly wasn't growing because of anything we'd done, and the previous homeowner must have cared for it well for it to be producing so much fruit. Those feelings reminded me of Jesus' words: "By this my Father is glorified, that you bear much fruit and so prove to be my disciples" (John 15:8). When our friends marveled at our healthy grapevine, we gave the credit to the previous homeowner. In the same way, when we do anything worthwhile, God is glorified, and it is evidence that we are His followers.

The result of the blessings of growth is astounding! Jesus is specific about what abiding in Him brings. He shares that when we abide, we receive an *extraordinary kind of love*, unlike anything this world offers (verse 9); and that we will have *indescribable joy* that is complete (verse 11). The Bible summarizes it perfectly: "Take root downward, and bear fruit upward" (2 Kings 19:30).

When we choose to take root in God and His Word, we will bear fruit upward to give Him glory. Abiding in Jesus is one incredible relationship!

Dead Branches

Over the years I've realized just how crucial my surrender is if I am to have a strong relationship with God. In my work, sometimes I've felt self-sufficient and confident in my abilities, with less than ideal results. In contrast, when I completely surrender all, I see God work in my life in mighty ways. This is so clear to me, it's hard not to be compelled to truly surrender to God, for His glory.

A little while ago I had a speaking appointment and was battling pride. In my journal I wrote:

> Lord, pride is one of my worst enemies. It seeks to take me away from needing You. Please humble me . . . I am Your servant today! Remove self from this picture. I am here to serve You alone. I surrender my life to You today. I surrender my will. I surrender my work—all of it. I surrender my future. I surrender my marriage—please continue to bless us! Be front and center of our relationship. I surrender my children—please help them to choose You today. I surrender my time—it is Yours. I surrender ALL to You, Lord. Send Your Holy Spirit to fall like rain into my life and my family today, please! I claim Isaiah 49:2 today:
> "And He has made My mouth" (Please bless my words today, Lord; and my writing)
> "Like a sharp sword; in the shadow of His hand He has hidden Me" (Draw me close to Your heart today, please)
> "And has made Me a polished shaft;" (Refine me, Lord, for your purposes, and keep me close)
> "In His quiver He has hidden Me."

Only when I come with open hands before the Lord, offering all and loving Him with every breath in my lungs, have I seen Him hold back the enemy and take the small, insignificant gifts He has given me and use them for His glory. Jesus surrendered all for us and made Himself a low servant to give us the option of a life with Him that never ends. What an incredible example of surrender!

When the Bible shows me things I need to surrender (like my pride), it's as though God is cutting off a dead branch from my life. It can be painful, and sometimes I want to keep those dead branches! But when I think back to our grapevine in Michigan, I know that if those seemingly dead branches had not grown leaves or fruit that summer, we would have cut them off. The dry sticks would have been evidence that there was no sap coursing through them.

Sometimes a branch can have a few dead parts that need to be removed. In the same way, our lives might have some branches that need pruning (John 15:1, 2). Our pride might cause a fall; our vanity might take a hit through a situation of some sort; or our selfish nature might need "trimming" in some way. Whatever way God allows us to be pruned causes us to become healthier as we abide in Him, particularly when it comes to producing the best possible fruit.

Nothing of any spiritual, eternal significance is possible apart from abiding in Jesus, the Vine. Jesus said it simply: "Whoever abides in me and I in him, he it is that bears much fruit, for apart from me you can do nothing" (John 15:5, ESV). Nothing! He didn't say we could partly abide and do a little by ourselves—no! We can do nothing of eternal significance without abiding in Christ.

I've seen this so much in my own life, and I can't state this point enough. In my family, church, work, and all areas of my life, unless I surrender completely, daily, moment by moment, all of my thoughts, my ideas, my desires to God; unless I ask Him to lead in every aspect of my life—if I withhold anything from Him, I can't expect Him to use my time, effort or work for His glory. And when I do surrender *all* to Him, He gives such an abundance! (John 10:10).

Bearing fruit requires a connection to the Vine first. It requires a complete surrender of self. God receives the glory when humans do the work that He could do by Himself if He chose to but gave it to us instead. Our utter dependence on the Vinedresser to manage the shape of our branches means completely trusting that He will prune when necessary.

It is allowing our fruit to be picked at the perfect time. It reveals that He allows us to have a time of regeneration before more fruit grows, showing that His care and timing are always perfect. He desires nothing more for you than to continue abiding in Him through His word.

9

Into Eternity

Heaven and earth will disappear,
but my words will never disappear.
Matthew 24:35, NLT

And there it is. The Word speaking truth into your heart, your life, and the lives of those around you. Have you found a "red chair" where you can meet God each day? What has changed in your life since you've been reading the Bible for yourself? How has bringing God's Word into your family changed your home?

It's easy to let a day, and then another day, slip by without spending time with the One who created the days and who gives us our time. It's easy to fill our lives so full of all the "important" things while subconsciously dismissing *the* most important thing—spending time with the God of the universe who wants to be close to you and to me.

The Bible tells us that a spiritual famine is nearly upon us:

> "Behold, the days are coming," says the Lord GOD,
> "That I will send a famine on the land,
> Not a famine of bread,
> Nor a thirst for water,
> But of hearing the words of the LORD.
> They shall wander from sea to sea,
> And from north to east;
> They shall run to and fro, seeking the word of the LORD,
> But shall not find it." (Amos 8:11, 12)

Right now, God's Word is accessible to you. You've tasted and seen how it can change things, both in your heart and in your family, and how easy it is to bring His Word into your life, even with just a few minutes each day. Will you covenant with God to bask in His Word into the future?

And you know what else? When we come thirsty to God's Word, our lives will be filled to overflowing. In one of my favorite chapters in the Bible, God promises that the word that goes forth from His mouth won't return to Him void. Read this chapter slowly and take in what God is telling you right now.

"Is anyone thirsty?
    Come and drink—
    even if you have no money!
Come, take your choice of wine or milk—
    it's all free!
Why spend your money on food that does not give you strength?
    Why pay for food that does you no good?
Listen to me, and you will eat what is good.
    You will enjoy the finest food.

"Come to me with your ears wide open.
    Listen, and you will find life.
I will make an everlasting covenant with you.
    I will give you all the unfailing love I promised to David.
See how I used him to display my power among the peoples.
    I made him a leader among the nations.
You also will command nations you do not know,
    and peoples unknown to you will come running to obey,
because I, the LORD your God,
    the Holy One of Israel, have made you glorious."

"Seek the LORD while you can find him.
    Call on him now while he is near.
Let the wicked change their ways
    and banish the very thought of doing wrong.
Let them turn to the LORD that he may have mercy on them.
    Yes, turn to our God, for he will forgive generously.

"My thoughts are nothing like your thoughts," says the LORD.
    "And my ways are far beyond anything you could imagine.

For just as the heavens are higher than the earth,
   so my ways are higher than your ways
   and my thoughts higher than your thoughts.

"The rain and snow come down from the heavens
   and stay on the ground to water the earth.
They cause the grain to grow,
   producing seed for the farmer
   and bread for the hungry.
It is the same with my word.
   I send it out, and it always produces fruit.
It will accomplish all I want it to,
   and it will prosper everywhere I send it.
You will live in joy and peace.
   The mountains and hills will burst into song,
   and the trees of the field will clap their hands!
Where once there were thorns, cypress trees will grow.
   Where nettles grew, myrtles will sprout up.
These events will bring great honor to the LORD's name;
   they will be an everlasting sign of his power and love."
   (Isaiah 55, NLT)

As you read the Word and let its light linger in your everyday life, God will continue to become better known to you. He will continue to speak truth into your life every day, even as you read and reread the same passages and stories over and over in the years to come.

And then one day soon, you'll see a small cloud growing bigger in the eastern sky, and your heart will know. It's Him. As He draws closer, your heart will race with expectation to the point where it nearly bursts with joy! You will see God, this Friend whom you've spent time with every day. Then you will see Him face-to-face. As you hear His voice ring out across the universe for the first time, you will know how right He was when He said, "Heaven and earth will disappear, but my words will never disappear" (Matthew 24:35, NLT). Yes, the words He speaks into our lives—His promises, the stories, our history as His people on this earth—will forever remind us of the impact of the Bible as a light that lingers in our lives for eternity.

Here are some examples of the POP (purpose of passage) cards.
You will see there are two different designs to choose from.
If you would like to print these, and others,
you can download them from **www.aslightlingers.com**

"For My people have committed two evils: They have forsaken Me, the fountain of living waters, And have hewn themselves cisterns—broken cisterns that can hold no water" (Jeremiah 2:13).

"Whoever dwells in the shelter
of the Most High
will rest in the shadow
of the Almighty.
I will say of the Lord,
'He is my refuge and fortress,
my God, in whom I trust.'
"Surely he will save you
from the fowler's snare
and from the deadly pestilence"
(Psalm 91:1 3, NIV).

" 'You are My witnesses,'
says the LORD,
'And my servant
whom I have chosen,
That you may know
and believe Me,
And understand
that I am He.
Before Me there was
no God formed,
Nor shall there be after Me.
I, even I, am the LORD,
And besides Me
there is no savior' "
(Isaiah 43:10, 11).

For I know
that my Redeemer lives,
And He shall stand
at last on the earth;
And after my skin is destroyed,
this I know,
That in my flesh I shall see God,
Whom I shall see for myself,
And my eyes shall behold,
and not another.
How my heart yearns
within me!"
(Job 19:25-27).

- When have you felt very hot and looked for a shadow to sit in?
- What would it be like to sit in God's shadow?
- These verses talk about resting in God's shadow. Why would you need to do that?
- What do these words make you think of? *refuge, fortress, snare, pestilence*
- How can God save you from these kinds of things in life?
- How can you stay in His shadow today?

- What is a cistern?
- What are the two evils that God talks about here?
- Do we also commit these two evils today? If so, how?
- What are some of the wells that you build?
- How can some wells "hold no water"?
- Do the wells that you build hold eternal significance?
- Why do people pursue broken, meaningless things, especially when living water is on tap for free?

- What is this passage talking about?
- Are you sure, like Job, that Jesus lives?
- Why is it important for Jesus to stand on this earth?
- Does this all seem a bit like a dream—a story you might have heard before that seems too good to be true? Why?
- How does your heart feel about this promise?

- What is this verse saying about us? About God?
- What does it mean to be God's witness, His servant, His chosen one?
- What is the difference between knowing, believing, and understanding God?
- When have you left God out of your life (maybe without even meaning to) to chase after worldly "gods" or things that take your time?
- This verse says that God is our only Savior. How does knowing this change the way you spend your time?

look, I go FORWARD but He is not there, and BACKWARD, but I cannot perceive Him; when He works on the LEFT HAND, I cannot behold Him; when He turns to the RIGHT HAND, I cannot see Him. BUT He knows the way that I take; When He has tested me, I shall come forth as GOLD

JOB 23:8-10

"for My THOUGHTS are not your THOUGHTS, Nor are your WAYS my WAYS, says the LORD. for as the HEAVENS are HIGHER than the EARTH, So are My WAYS higher than your ways and My THOUGHTS than your THOUGHTS."

ISAIAH 55:8+9

YOU ARE MY LAMP O LORD; the LORD shall ENLIGHTEN my darkness. As for God, His way is PERFECT; the WORD of the Lord is PROVEN; He is a SHIELD to all who TRUST in Him.

2 SAMUEL 22:29,31

Let NOT your HEART be troubled; you BELIEVE in God, believe also in ME. In My FATHER'S HOUSE are many MANSIONS; if it were not so, I would have told you. I go to prepare a PLACE for YOU. And if I go & PREPARE a place for you I WILL come again and RECEIVE you to MYSELF; that where I am, there you may be also. And where I go you know, & the way you know.

JOHN 14:1-4

- Have you ever looked at the stars at night and wondered how far up heaven is?

- What might it be like for God to look all the way down to earth from heaven?

- Why are God's thoughts different from our thoughts?

- What does this verse mean to us today? Why might we need to be reminded of this?

- What is Job talking about here?

- Have you ever wondered whether God is really still there? When?

- In what ways might God test us, as Job suggests?

- How can we become like gold? What does that mean?

- How can this passage encourage you today?

- What is one thing you're most looking forward to about heaven?

- What kinds of things are troubling your heart at the moment?

- On a scale of one being very easy, and five being very difficult, how easy or difficult do you find it to believe in God and what He has said?

- What kind of place do you think Jesus is preparing for you right now? (For more details, see Revelation 21–22.)

- What kind of God cares so deeply for humankind that He would use all measures to secure our future in heaven with Him?

- Have you ever been afraid of the dark?

- What makes the dark scary?

- How could God be our lamp?

- When have you doubted that God's way is perfect?

- When have you trusted in God's way?

- What do you need God to shield you from today?

BIG QUESTIONS

1. What does this passage tell me about **God**?

2. What does this passage tell me about **myself and humanity**?

3. What **change** will I make today as a result of understanding God's word?

4. What does this passage or story tell me about the **great controversy between good and evil**?

5. Where can I see the **work of redemption** (God saving humankind) in this passage or story?

6. What **other passages** can I find that further expand on these themes?

As *Light Lingers*

Basking in the Word of God.

by *Nina Atcheson*

CLAIMING PROMISES AS MY PERSONAL PRAYERS

- **God's love for me, a sinner:**
  Hosea 11; John 3:16, 17; Jude 24, 25

- **Assurance that God is leading:**
  Daniel 2:20–23; Ecclesiastes 3:1–15; Psalm 31

- **Feeling lonely or sad:**
  Matthew 5:3–12; Philippians 4:4–8; 4:19

- **Guidance on how to live:**
  Jeremiah 31:33; Exodus 20; Micah 6:8; 1 Corinthians 13; Colossians 3:12–17

- **Praising God:**
  Psalm 67; Job 37

- **Feeling stressed or worried:**
  Luke 12:22–34; Hebrews 13:5, 6; 1 Peter 5:6, 7

- **Living like a Christian:**
  Romans 12:9–21; Ephesians 5:8–14; 1 John 1:7; 2:15–17

As *Light Lingers*

Basking in the Word of God.

by *Nina Atcheson*

CLAIMING PROMISES AS MY PERSONAL PRAYERS

- **Seeking wisdom from God:**
  Proverbs 2:1–9

- **Feeling scared:**
  Psalm 91; 57:1–3

- **Fighting the enemy:**
  Ephesians 6:10–20; 1 Peter 5:8–11

- **Wanting to repent:**
  Psalm 51; 2 Timothy 2:19–22

- **Realizing I am in need of a Savior:**
  John 6:41–51; Ephesians 2:4–10

- **Seeking Jesus more:**
  Jeremiah 24:7; 29:11–14

- **God is more powerful than my circumstances:**
  Isaiah 55; Zephaniah 3:16, 17

- **Needing to fix my eyes on eternity rather than what is before me:**
  Isaiah 65:17–25; 1 Thessalonians 4:15–18; Revelation 21; 22

- **Needing boldness to speak for God:**
  Isaiah 55:11; 59:21; 2 Timothy 1:8–12; 4:2–5; 1 Peter 3:13–17

- **For healing (spiritual or physical):**
  Isaiah 58:8; 2 Corinthians 4:16–18; James 5:13–16

As *Light* Lingers
Basking in the Word of God.
by Nina Atcheson

WHO, WHERE, WHEN, WHAT, WHY?

WHO are the key people in this story or passage? (What do they tell me?)

WHERE did this story take place? (How might knowing the location add to the story?)

WHEN did this happen in relation to other big events in the Bible? (What is the context of the story?)

WHAT happened in this story? (What is the big message of this story?)

WHY might this story or passage have been included in the Bible? (What does it say to me today?)

As *Light* Lingers
Basking in the Word of God.
by Nina Atcheson

BOOK OR CHAPTER STUDY

1. **PRAY:** Before you begin, pray for the Holy Spirit to guide your mind and your heart as you read.
2. **READ:** As you slowly read the chapter, underline any big ideas that stand out to you.
3. **REFLECT AND REWRITE:** Reflect on the verses and ideas you've underlined, and rewrite these in your journal.
4. **RELATE:** What is God saying directly to you through this passage? Reflect and respond in your journal.
5. **PRAY:** Write a personal prayer response to God.

VERSE-BY-VERSE

1. **Pray** for the Holy Spirit to guide your mind and heart as you read.
2. **Choose** a Bible verse or passage.
3. **Write the passage** in your journal. Then read it aloud.
4. Find one **big idea** in the verse. **Underline** it in your journal.
5. What is the big idea telling you about **God or yourself**? Write your thoughts in your journal.
6. What do you want to say to God? **Write your thoughts as a prayer** in your journal.

KID'S BIBLE STUDY GUIDE

1. **Ask Jesus** to be with you as you read.
2. **Choose** a Bible verse or passage.
3. **Write the passage** in your journal. Then read it aloud.
4. **Underline the big idea** in the passage.
5. Write down **what the big idea tells you about God or yourself.**
6. Write down (or whisper) a prayer of what you **want to say to Jesus.**

Tahlia A

As *Light Lingers*
Basking in the Word of God.
by *Nina Aitcheson*

You have been taught the holy Scriptures from childhood, and they have given you the wisdom to receive the salvation that comes by trusting in Christ Jesus. All Scripture is inspired by God and is useful to teach us what is true and to make us realize what is wrong in our lives.

2 Timothy 3:15-16 (NLT)

Tahlia A

WORD STUDY

1. **Pray** for the Holy Spirit to guide your mind and heart as you read.

2. Write out the **same verse multiple times**.

3. Consider the **different words** in the verse.

4. Write your thoughts about **what these words are saying** to you today.

5. Write a **prayer response** to God.

"The study of the Bible demands our most diligent effort and perse vering thought. As the miner digs for the golden treasure in the earth, so earnestly, persistently, must we seek for the treasure of God's word."

Ellen G. White, *Education, p. 189*

As *Light* *Lingers*
Basking in the Word of God.
by Nina Atcheson

As *Light* *Lingers*
Basking in the Word of God.
by Nina Atcheson

As *Light* *Lingers*
Basking in the Word of God.
by Nina Atcheson